THE ESSENTIAL
CRYING
BABY
WORKBOOK

LOWELL HOUSE
PRESS

www.essentialcryingbabybook.com

ISBN: 978-0-9991625-2-1

Printed in the United States of America

www.essentialcryingbabybook.com

ks@drkristinesmith.com

only the most difficult challenges in life
lead to meaningful rewards

-KRISTINE SMITH

Contents

Hey there mama...

In *The Essential Crying Baby Book: Support and Resources to Help You Cope With Colic and Calm Your Fussy Baby*, we talk a lot about feeling tired, overwhelmed, and helpless when your baby won't stop crying. It's not easy to raise a newborn - but caring for a newborn that is excessively fussy, or has colic, is exceptionally difficult. As emphasized in *The Essential Crying Baby Book* it is crucial to work with your pediatrician to rule out potential medical causes of crying, feeding or digestive problems, or sleep issues. Furthermore, it's so helpful to have information at your fingertips regarding your baby's behavioral patterns when meeting with your pediatrician. Unfortunately, it can be hard to remember what happened five minutes ago let alone last week when you are a sleep-deprived, harried new mom. The goal of this workbook is to help you keep track of your baby's daily (and weekly) crying, sleeping, feeding and digestive patterns so you can reflect upon them yourself, and also discuss with your pediatrician, nurses, lactation specialists and family members.

Scientific evidence shows that several things are important to our mental well-being, including feeling grateful for the good things in our life, having self-compassion and caring for ourselves, deep connections to others through expressing our feelings and vulnerabilities openly and honestly, and giving and receiving help from others. Challenges to maternal mental health and wellness are some of the most common families face – and they can easily be overlooked by doctors, friends and family, even us. To serve as a reminder of the importance of caring for yourself, this workbook has daily prompts for gratitude, rewarding yourself, getting feelings and concerns off your chest, and reaching out for help. Please know it is completely normal to feel unhappy at times. You *can* do this. *But you shouldn't have to do it alone.* Asking for help or support, whether it be a little or a lot, makes for a good mom – and that's exactly what you are!

INSTRUCTIONS

How to use this workbook:

This workbook, although derived from my personal struggle with a colicky baby, has been designed to help moms with a variety of newborn challenges. Keeping track of food trials? Feedings? Doctor visits? Crying patterns? Soothing techniques? Whatever it is for you, we've left plenty of space to focus on and take extra notes for yourself and your doctor on your biggest area of concern.

The *Daily Log Chart* makes it easy for you to keep track of key events and behavioral patterns throughout each day with a simple mark of a pen. At each hour, you can mark your baby's *main activity* over the previous 60 minutes, or you can make marks between hours. Record any vomiting episodes, diaper changes, feedings, crying fits, naps, at their estimated time on your chart. Feel free to draw continuous lines from one time to another (for example, a nap that lasts from 4pm-6pm), make notes right on the chart (pees and poops, etc.), whatever you choose!

The *Daily Log Record* allows you to look over your completed *Daily Log Chart* and summarize any patterns (for example, infant crying for more than three hours a day, more than three days a week, for over three weeks is a common criteria for diagnosing colic), digestive problems (e.g., frequent vomiting and when it occurs), etc.—and make note of any concerns you have. You may want to summarize each day's events the following morning, since we have created the *Daily Log Chart* to extend into overnight hours. The *Daily Log Record* is also meant to give you reminders to take care of yourself and pay attention to how you are feeling. A healthy mama makes for a healthy baby. However, if there are other reminders that would work better for you, cross ours out and write in your own!

At the end of each seven day period there is a *Weekly Summary Sheet* for you to keep track of what happened over the past week and have a condensed review. The *Pediatric Visit Logs* are included to help you retain memory of key observations and concerns from your *Weekly Summary Sheets* to frame questions for your pediatrician. You are able to record those questions for your next upcoming pediatric visit beforehand so that you don't forget them during those time-pressured doctor's appointments!

We've included some *Journal Pages* near the end of this Workbook for you to vent frustrations, record how you are feeling, visualize your wonderful future with your baby, whatever you have to say or get off your chest. Likewise, the *Extra Notes Pages* at the end provide extra space to use as you see fit. We'd love to hear from you how you have used this Workbook, how it has helped you and suggestions for future changes. Consider joining the **Essential Crying Baby Book** Community to receive more information, support and share your story at www.essentialcryingbabybook.com.

With Love,

Kristine

2017

January
Mo	Tu	We	Th	Fr	Sa	Su
						1
2	3	4	5	6	7	8
9	10	11	12	13	14	15
16	17	18	19	20	21	22
23	24	25	26	27	28	29
30	31					

February
Mo	Tu	We	Th	Fr	Sa	Su
		1	2	3	4	5
6	7	8	9	10	11	12
13	14	15	16	17	18	19
20	21	22	23	24	25	26
27	28					

March
Mo	Tu	We	Th	Fr	Sa	Su
		1	2	3	4	5
6	7	8	9	10	11	12
13	14	15	16	17	18	19
20	21	22	23	24	25	26
27	28	29	30	31		

April
Mo	Tu	We	Th	Fr	Sa	Su
					1	2
3	4	5	6	7	8	9
10	11	12	13	14	15	16
17	18	19	20	21	22	23
24	25	26	27	28	29	30

May
Mo	Tu	We	Th	Fr	Sa	Su
1	2	3	4	5	6	7
8	9	10	11	12	13	14
15	16	17	18	19	20	21
22	23	24	25	26	27	28
29	30	31				

June
Mo	Tu	We	Th	Fr	Sa	Su
			1	2	3	4
5	6	7	8	9	10	11
12	13	14	15	16	17	18
19	20	21	22	23	24	25
26	27	28	29	30		

July
Mo	Tu	We	Th	Fr	Sa	Su
					1	2
3	4	5	6	7	8	9
10	11	12	13	14	15	16
17	18	19	20	21	22	23
24	25	26	27	28	29	30
31						

August
Mo	Tu	We	Th	Fr	Sa	Su
	1	2	3	4	5	6
7	8	9	10	11	12	13
14	15	16	17	18	19	20
21	22	23	24	25	26	27
28	29	30	31			

September
Mo	Tu	We	Th	Fr	Sa	Su
				1	2	3
4	5	6	7	8	9	10
11	12	13	14	15	16	17
18	19	20	21	22	23	24
25	26	27	28	29	30	

October
Mo	Tu	We	Th	Fr	Sa	Su
						1
2	3	4	5	6	7	8
9	10	11	12	13	14	15
16	17	18	19	20	21	22
23	24	25	26	27	28	29
30	31					

November
Mo	Tu	We	Th	Fr	Sa	Su
		1	2	3	4	5
6	7	8	9	10	11	12
13	14	15	16	17	18	19
20	21	22	23	24	25	26
27	28	29	30			

December
Mo	Tu	We	Th	Fr	Sa	Su
				1	2	3
4	5	6	7	8	9	10
11	12	13	14	15	16	17
18	19	20	21	22	23	24
25	26	27	28	29	30	31

2018

January
Mo	Tu	We	Th	Fr	Sa	Su
1	2	3	4	5	6	7
8	9	10	11	12	13	14
15	16	17	18	19	20	21
22	23	24	25	26	27	28
29	30	31				

February
Mo	Tu	We	Th	Fr	Sa	Su
			1	2	3	4
5	6	7	8	9	10	11
12	13	14	15	16	17	18
19	20	21	22	23	24	25
26	27	28				

March
Mo	Tu	We	Th	Fr	Sa	Su
			1	2	3	4
5	6	7	8	9	10	11
12	13	14	15	16	17	18
19	20	21	22	23	24	25
26	27	28	29	30	31	

April
Mo	Tu	We	Th	Fr	Sa	Su
						1
2	3	4	5	6	7	8
9	10	11	12	13	14	15
16	17	18	19	20	21	22
23	24	25	26	27	28	29
30						

May
Mo	Tu	We	Th	Fr	Sa	Su
	1	2	3	4	5	6
7	8	9	10	11	12	13
14	15	16	17	18	19	20
21	22	23	24	25	26	27
28	29	30	31			

June
Mo	Tu	We	Th	Fr	Sa	Su
				1	2	3
4	5	6	7	8	9	10
11	12	13	14	15	16	17
18	19	20	21	22	23	24
25	26	27	28	29	30	

July
Mo	Tu	We	Th	Fr	Sa	Su
						1
2	3	4	5	6	7	8
9	10	11	12	13	14	15
16	17	18	19	20	21	22
23	24	25	26	27	28	29
30	31					

August
Mo	Tu	We	Th	Fr	Sa	Su
		1	2	3	4	5
6	7	8	9	10	11	12
13	14	15	16	17	18	19
20	21	22	23	24	25	26
27	28	29	30	31		

September
Mo	Tu	We	Th	Fr	Sa	Su
					1	2
3	4	5	6	7	8	9
10	11	12	13	14	15	16
17	18	19	20	21	22	23
24	25	26	27	28	29	30

October
Mo	Tu	We	Th	Fr	Sa	Su
1	2	3	4	5	6	7
8	9	10	11	12	13	14
15	16	17	18	19	20	21
22	23	24	25	26	27	28
29	30	31				

November
Mo	Tu	We	Th	Fr	Sa	Su
			1	2	3	4
5	6	7	8	9	10	11
12	13	14	15	16	17	18
19	20	21	22	23	24	25
26	27	28	29	30		

December
Mo	Tu	We	Th	Fr	Sa	Su
					1	2
3	4	5	6	7	8	9
10	11	12	13	14	15	16
17	18	19	20	21	22	23
24	25	26	27	28	29	30
31						

2019

January
Mo	Tu	We	Th	Fr	Sa	Su
	1	2	3	4	5	6
7	8	9	10	11	12	13
14	15	16	17	18	19	20
21	22	23	24	25	26	27
28	29	30	31			

February
Mo	Tu	We	Th	Fr	Sa	Su
				1	2	3
4	5	6	7	8	9	10
11	12	13	14	15	16	17
18	19	20	21	22	23	24
25	26	27	28			

March
Mo	Tu	We	Th	Fr	Sa	Su
				1	2	3
4	5	6	7	8	9	10
11	12	13	14	15	16	17
18	19	20	21	22	23	24
25	26	27	28	29	30	31

April
Mo	Tu	We	Th	Fr	Sa	Su
1	2	3	4	5	6	7
8	9	10	11	12	13	14
15	16	17	18	19	20	21
22	23	24	25	26	27	28
29	30					

May
Mo	Tu	We	Th	Fr	Sa	Su
	1	2	3	4	5	
6	7	8	9	10	11	12
13	14	15	16	17	18	19
20	21	22	23	24	25	26
27	28	29	30	31		

June
Mo	Tu	We	Th	Fr	Sa	Su
					1	2
3	4	5	6	7	8	9
10	11	12	13	14	15	16
17	18	19	20	21	22	23
24	25	26	27	28	29	30

July
Mo	Tu	We	Th	Fr	Sa	Su
1	2	3	4	5	6	7
8	9	10	11	12	13	14
15	16	17	18	19	20	21
22	23	24	25	26	27	28
29	30	31				

August
Mo	Tu	We	Th	Fr	Sa	Su
			1	2	3	4
5	6	7	8	9	10	11
12	13	14	15	16	17	18
19	20	21	22	23	24	25
26	27	28	29	30	31	

September
Mo	Tu	We	Th	Fr	Sa	Su
						1
2	3	4	5	6	7	8
9	10	11	12	13	14	15
16	17	18	19	20	21	22
23	24	25	26	27	28	29
30						

October
Mo	Tu	We	Th	Fr	Sa	Su
	1	2	3	4	5	6
7	8	9	10	11	12	13
14	15	16	17	18	19	20
21	22	23	24	25	26	27
28	29	30	31			

November
Mo	Tu	We	Th	Fr	Sa	Su
				1	2	3
4	5	6	7	8	9	10
11	12	13	14	15	16	17
18	19	20	21	22	23	24
25	26	27	28	29	30	

December
Mo	Tu	We	Th	Fr	Sa	Su
						1
2	3	4	5	6	7	8
9	10	11	12	13	14	15
16	17	18	19	20	21	22
23	24	25	26	27	28	29
30	31					

2020

January
Mo	Tu	We	Th	Fr	Sa	Su
	1	2	3	4	5	
6	7	8	9	10	11	12
13	14	15	16	17	18	19
20	21	22	23	24	25	26
27	28	29	30	31		

February
Mo	Tu	We	Th	Fr	Sa	Su
					1	2
3	4	5	6	7	8	9
10	11	12	13	14	15	16
17	18	19	20	21	22	23
24	25	26	27	28	29	

March
Mo	Tu	We	Th	Fr	Sa	Su
						1
2	3	4	5	6	7	8
9	10	11	12	13	14	15
16	17	18	19	20	21	22
23	24	25	26	27	28	29
30	31					

April
Mo	Tu	We	Th	Fr	Sa	Su
		1	2	3	4	5
6	7	8	9	10	11	12
13	14	15	16	17	18	19
20	21	22	23	24	25	26
27	28	29	30			

May
Mo	Tu	We	Th	Fr	Sa	Su
				1	2	3
4	5	6	7	8	9	10
11	12	13	14	15	16	17
18	19	20	21	22	23	24
25	26	27	28	29	30	31

June
Mo	Tu	We	Th	Fr	Sa	Su
1	2	3	4	5	6	7
8	9	10	11	12	13	14
15	16	17	18	19	20	21
22	23	24	25	26	27	28
29	30					

July
Mo	Tu	We	Th	Fr	Sa	Su
		1	2	3	4	5
6	7	8	9	10	11	12
13	14	15	16	17	18	19
20	21	22	23	24	25	26
27	28	29	30	31		

August
Mo	Tu	We	Th	Fr	Sa	Su
					1	2
3	4	5	6	7	8	9
10	11	12	13	14	15	16
17	18	19	20	21	22	23
24	25	26	27	28	29	30
31						

September
Mo	Tu	We	Th	Fr	Sa	Su
	1	2	3	4	5	6
7	8	9	10	11	12	13
14	15	16	17	18	19	20
21	22	23	24	25	26	27
28	29	30				

October
Mo	Tu	We	Th	Fr	Sa	Su
			1	2	3	4
5	6	7	8	9	10	11
12	13	14	15	16	17	18
19	20	21	22	23	24	25
26	27	28	29	30	31	

November
Mo	Tu	We	Th	Fr	Sa	Su
						1
2	3	4	5	6	7	8
9	10	11	12	13	14	15
16	17	18	19	20	21	22
23	24	25	26	27	28	29
30						

December
Mo	Tu	We	Th	Fr	Sa	Su
	1	2	3	4	5	6
7	8	9	10	11	12	13
14	15	16	17	18	19	20
21	22	23	24	25	26	27
28	29	30	31			

WEEK ONE

Daily Log Record

Date: _____   Day of the Week: _____

What I'm grateful for today:

How I'm going to care for/reward myself today:

How am I feeling today?

Current food trials (if any):

Number of days my baby or I have been avoiding this food:

Daily Log Chart Summary

(fill this out after today's chart on the next page is complete)

Total estimated crying time today:
Any concerns?

Total estimated sleeping time:
Any concerns?

Total number of vomiting episodes:
Any concerns?

Daily Log Chart

	Feeding	Diaper change	Vomiting	Spit-up	Extreme Crying	Crying	Moderate fussiness	Mild fussiness	Content	Sleeping
5:00 AM										
6:00 AM										
7:00 AM										
8:00 AM										
9:00 AM										
10:00 AM										
11:00 AM										
12:00 PM										
1:00 PM										
2:00 PM										
3:00 PM										
4:00 PM										
5:00 PM										
6:00 PM										
7:00 PM										
8:00 PM										
9:00 PM										
10:00 PM										
11:00 PM										
12:00 AM										
1:00 AM										
2:00 AM										
3:00 AM										
4:00 AM										

INSTRUCTIONS: Place a mark each hour to denote what your baby's main mood was over the previous hour. Place a mark at the estimated times of spit-ups, vomiting, feedings, or diaper changes. *Make additional notes below.*

Daily Log Record

Date: _____   Day of the Week: _____

What I'm grateful for today:

How I'm going to care for/reward myself today:

How am I feeling today?

Current food trials (if any):

Number of days my baby or I have been avoiding this food:

Daily Log Chart Summary

(fill this out after today's chart on the next page is complete)

Total estimated crying time today:
Any concerns?

Total estimated sleeping time:
Any concerns?

Total number of vomiting episodes:
Any concerns?

DAILY LOG CHART

	Feeding	Diaper change	Vomiting	Spit-up	Extreme Crying	Crying	Moderate fussiness	Mild fussiness	Content	Sleeping
5:00 AM										
6:00 AM										
7:00 AM										
8:00 AM										
9:00 AM										
10:00 AM										
11:00 AM										
12:00 PM										
1:00 PM										
2:00 PM										
3:00 PM										
4:00 PM										
5:00 PM										
6:00 PM										
7:00 PM										
8:00 PM										
9:00 PM										
10:00 PM										
11:00 PM										
12:00 AM										
1:00 AM										
2:00 AM										
3:00 AM										
4:00 AM										

INSTRUCTIONS: Place a mark each hour to denote what your baby's main mood was over the previous hour. Place a mark at the estimated times of spit-ups, vomiting, feedings, or diaper changes. *Make additional notes below.*

Daily Log Record

Date: _____ Day of the Week: _____

What I'm grateful for today:

How I'm going to care for/reward myself today:

How am I feeling today?

Current food trials (if any):

Number of days my baby or I have been avoiding this food:

Daily Log Chart Summary

(fill this out after today's chart on the next page is complete)

Total estimated crying time today:
Any concerns?

Total estimated sleeping time:
Any concerns?

Total number of vomiting episodes:
Any concerns?

Daily Log Chart

	Feeding	Diaper change	Vomiting	Spit-up	Extreme Crying	Crying	Moderate fussiness	Mild fussiness	Content	Sleeping
5:00 AM										
6:00 AM										
7:00 AM										
8:00 AM										
9:00 AM										
10:00 AM										
11:00 AM										
12:00 PM										
1:00 PM										
2:00 PM										
3:00 PM										
4:00 PM										
5:00 PM										
6:00 PM										
7:00 PM										
8:00 PM										
9:00 PM										
10:00 PM										
11:00 PM										
12:00 AM										
1:00 AM										
2:00 AM										
3:00 AM										
4:00 AM										

INSTRUCTIONS: Place a mark each hour to denote what your baby's main mood was over the previous hour. Place a mark at the estimated times of spit-ups, vomiting, feedings, or diaper changes. *Make additional notes below.*

Daily Log Record

Date: _____   Day of the Week: _____

What I'm grateful for today:

How I'm going to care for/reward myself today:

How am I feeling today?

Current food trials (if any):

Number of days my baby or I have been avoiding this food:

Daily Log Chart Summary

(fill this out after today's chart on the next page is complete)

Total estimated crying time today:
Any concerns?

Total estimated sleeping time:
Any concerns?

Total number of vomiting episodes:
Any concerns?

DAILY LOG CHART

	Feeding	Diaper change	Vomiting	Spit-up	Extreme Crying	Crying	Moderate fussiness	Mild fussiness	Content	Sleeping
5:00 AM										
6:00 AM										
7:00 AM										
8:00 AM										
9:00 AM										
10:00 AM										
11:00 AM										
12:00 PM										
1:00 PM										
2:00 PM										
3:00 PM										
4:00 PM										
5:00 PM										
6:00 PM										
7:00 PM										
8:00 PM										
9:00 PM										
10:00 PM										
11:00 PM										
12:00 AM										
1:00 AM										
2:00 AM										
3:00 AM										
4:00 AM										

INSTRUCTIONS: Place a mark each hour to denote what your baby's main mood was over the previous hour. Place a mark at the estimated times of spit-ups, vomiting, feedings, or diaper changes. *Make additional notes below.*

Daily Log Record

Date: _____   Day of the Week: _____

What I'm grateful for today:

How I'm going to care for/reward myself today:

How am I feeling today?

Current food trials (if any):

Number of days my baby or I have been avoiding this food:

Daily Log Chart Summary

(fill this out after today's chart on the next page is complete)

Total estimated crying time today:
Any concerns?

Total estimated sleeping time:
Any concerns?

Total number of vomiting episodes:
Any concerns?

Daily Log Chart

	Feeding	Diaper change	Vomiting	Spit-up	Extreme Crying	Crying	Moderate fussiness	Mild fussiness	Content	Sleeping
5:00 AM										
6:00 AM										
7:00 AM										
8:00 AM										
9:00 AM										
10:00 AM										
11:00 AM										
12:00 PM										
1:00 PM										
2:00 PM										
3:00 PM										
4:00 PM										
5:00 PM										
6:00 PM										
7:00 PM										
8:00 PM										
9:00 PM										
10:00 PM										
11:00 PM										
12:00 AM										
1:00 AM										
2:00 AM										
3:00 AM										
4:00 AM										

INSTRUCTIONS: Place a mark each hour to denote what your baby's main mood was over the previous hour. Place a mark at the estimated times of spit-ups, vomiting, feedings, or diaper changes. *Make additional notes below.*

Daily Log Record

Date: _____   Day of the Week: _____

What I'm grateful for today:

How I'm going to care for/reward myself today:

How am I feeling today?

Current food trials (if any):

Number of days my baby or I have been avoiding this food:

Daily Log Chart Summary

(fill this out after today's chart on the next page is complete)

Total estimated crying time today:
Any concerns?

Total estimated sleeping time:
Any concerns?

Total number of vomiting episodes:
Any concerns?

Daily Log Chart

	Feeding	Diaper change	Vomiting	Spit-up	Extreme Crying	Crying	Moderate fussiness	Mild fussiness	Content	Sleeping
5:00 AM										
6:00 AM										
7:00 AM										
8:00 AM										
9:00 AM										
10:00 AM										
11:00 AM										
12:00 PM										
1:00 PM										
2:00 PM										
3:00 PM										
4:00 PM										
5:00 PM										
6:00 PM										
7:00 PM										
8:00 PM										
9:00 PM										
10:00 PM										
11:00 PM										
12:00 AM										
1:00 AM										
2:00 AM										
3:00 AM										
4:00 AM										

INSTRUCTIONS: Place a mark each hour to denote what your baby's main mood was over the previous hour. Place a mark at the estimated times of spit-ups, vomiting, feedings, or diaper changes. *Make additional notes below.*

Daily Log Record

Date: _____ Day of the Week: _____

What I'm grateful for today:

How I'm going to care for/reward myself today:

How am I feeling today?

Current food trials (if any):

Number of days my baby or I have been avoiding this food:

Daily Log Chart Summary

(fill this out after today's chart on the next page is complete)

Total estimated crying time today:
Any concerns?

Total estimated sleeping time:
Any concerns?

Total number of vomiting episodes:
Any concerns?

DAILY LOG CHART

	Feeding	Diaper change	Vomiting	Spit-up	Extreme Crying	Crying	Moderate fussiness	Mild fussiness	Content	Sleeping
5:00 AM										
6:00 AM										
7:00 AM										
8:00 AM										
9:00 AM										
10:00 AM										
11:00 AM										
12:00 PM										
1:00 PM										
2:00 PM										
3:00 PM										
4:00 PM										
5:00 PM										
6:00 PM										
7:00 PM										
8:00 PM										
9:00 PM										
10:00 PM										
11:00 PM										
12:00 AM										
1:00 AM										
2:00 AM										
3:00 AM										
4:00 AM										

INSTRUCTIONS: Place a mark each hour to denote what your baby's main mood was over the previous hour. Place a mark at the estimated times of spit-ups, vomiting, feedings, or diaper changes. *Make additional notes below.*

"speak your truth"

Weekly Summary Sheet

My baby's age (in weeks):

What was the highlight (best thing that happened) this week?

Observations of my baby's crying behavior this week (e.g., how many hours on average per day did my baby cry? What time of day? Did the crying seem to correlate with certain needs or events?)

Observations of my baby's feeding and digestive patterns this week (including latching, feeding, vomiting issues, etc.):

Notes/questions from this week to remember for my pediatrician or lactation specialist:

Any lessons I need to remember from this week? (e.g., what activities did my baby seem to enjoy most?)

What I'm going to ask for more help with next week:

WEEK TWO

Daily Log Record

Date: _____   Day of the Week: _____

What I'm grateful for today:

How I'm going to care for/reward myself today:

How am I feeling today?

Current food trials (if any):

Number of days my baby or I have been avoiding this food:

Daily Log Chart Summary

(fill this out after today's chart on the next page is complete)

Total estimated crying time today:
Any concerns?

Total estimated sleeping time:
Any concerns?

Total number of vomiting episodes:
Any concerns?

Daily Log Chart

	Feeding	Diaper change	Vomiting	Spit-up	Extreme Crying	Crying	Moderate fussiness	Mild fussiness	Content	Sleeping
5:00 AM										
6:00 AM										
7:00 AM										
8:00 AM										
9:00 AM										
10:00 AM										
11:00 AM										
12:00 PM										
1:00 PM										
2:00 PM										
3:00 PM										
4:00 PM										
5:00 PM										
6:00 PM										
7:00 PM										
8:00 PM										
9:00 PM										
10:00 PM										
11:00 PM										
12:00 AM										
1:00 AM										
2:00 AM										
3:00 AM										
4:00 AM										

INSTRUCTIONS: Place a mark each hour to denote what your baby's main mood was over the previous hour. Place a mark at the estimated times of spit-ups, vomiting, feedings, or diaper changes. *Make additional notes below.*

DAILY LOG RECORD

Date: _____ Day of the Week: _____

What I'm grateful for today:

How I'm going to care for/reward myself today:

How am I feeling today?

Current food trials (if any):

Number of days my baby or I have been avoiding this food:

DAILY LOG CHART SUMMARY

(fill this out after today's chart on the next page is complete)

Total estimated crying time today:
Any concerns?

Total estimated sleeping time:
Any concerns?

Total number of vomiting episodes:
Any concerns?

Daily Log Chart

	Feeding	Diaper change	Vomiting	Spit-up	Extreme Crying	Crying	Moderate fussiness	Mild fussiness	Content	Sleeping
5:00 AM										
6:00 AM										
7:00 AM										
8:00 AM										
9:00 AM										
10:00 AM										
11:00 AM										
12:00 PM										
1:00 PM										
2:00 PM										
3:00 PM										
4:00 PM										
5:00 PM										
6:00 PM										
7:00 PM										
8:00 PM										
9:00 PM										
10:00 PM										
11:00 PM										
12:00 AM										
1:00 AM										
2:00 AM										
3:00 AM										
4:00 AM										

INSTRUCTIONS: Place a mark each hour to denote what your baby's main mood was over the previous hour. Place a mark at the estimated times of spit-ups, vomiting, feedings, or diaper changes. *Make additional notes below.*

Daily Log Record

Date: _____   Day of the Week: _____

What I'm grateful for today:

How I'm going to care for/reward myself today:

How am I feeling today?

Current food trials (if any):

Number of days my baby or I have been avoiding this food:

Daily Log Chart Summary

(fill this out after today's chart on the next page is complete)

Total estimated crying time today:
Any concerns?

Total estimated sleeping time:
Any concerns?

Total number of vomiting episodes:
Any concerns?

Daily Log Chart

	Feeding	Diaper change	Vomiting	Spit-up	Extreme Crying	Crying	Moderate fussiness	Mild fussiness	Content	Sleeping
5:00 AM										
6:00 AM										
7:00 AM										
8:00 AM										
9:00 AM										
10:00 AM										
11:00 AM										
12:00 PM										
1:00 PM										
2:00 PM										
3:00 PM										
4:00 PM										
5:00 PM										
6:00 PM										
7:00 PM										
8:00 PM										
9:00 PM										
10:00 PM										
11:00 PM										
12:00 AM										
1:00 AM										
2:00 AM										
3:00 AM										
4:00 AM										

INSTRUCTIONS: Place a mark each hour to denote what your baby's main mood was over the previous hour. Place a mark at the estimated times of spit-ups, vomiting, feedings, or diaper changes. *Make additional notes below.*

Daily Log Record

Date: _____   Day of the Week: _____

What I'm grateful for today:

How I'm going to care for/reward myself today:

How am I feeling today?

Current food trials (if any):

Number of days my baby or I have been avoiding this food:

Daily Log Chart Summary

(fill this out after today's chart on the next page is complete)

Total estimated crying time today:
Any concerns?

Total estimated sleeping time:
Any concerns?

Total number of vomiting episodes:
Any concerns?

Daily Log Chart

	Feeding	Diaper change	Vomiting	Spit-up	Extreme Crying	Crying	Moderate fussiness	Mild fussiness	Content	Sleeping
5:00 AM										
6:00 AM										
7:00 AM										
8:00 AM										
9:00 AM										
10:00 AM										
11:00 AM										
12:00 PM										
1:00 PM										
2:00 PM										
3:00 PM										
4:00 PM										
5:00 PM										
6:00 PM										
7:00 PM										
8:00 PM										
9:00 PM										
10:00 PM										
11:00 PM										
12:00 AM										
1:00 AM										
2:00 AM										
3:00 AM										
4:00 AM										

INSTRUCTIONS: Place a mark each hour to denote what your baby's main mood was over the previous hour. Place a mark at the estimated times of spit-ups, vomiting, feedings, or diaper changes. *Make additional notes below.*

DAILY LOG RECORD

Date: _____   Day of the Week: _____

What I'm grateful for today:

How I'm going to care for/reward myself today:

How am I feeling today?

Current food trials (if any):

Number of days my baby or I have been avoiding this food:

DAILY LOG CHART SUMMARY

(fill this out after today's chart on the next page is complete)

Total estimated crying time today:
Any concerns?

Total estimated sleeping time:
Any concerns?

Total number of vomiting episodes:
Any concerns?

Daily Log Chart

	Feeding	Diaper change	Vomiting	Spit-up	Extreme Crying	Crying	Moderate fussiness	Mild fussiness	Content	Sleeping
5:00 AM										
6:00 AM										
7:00 AM										
8:00 AM										
9:00 AM										
10:00 AM										
11:00 AM										
12:00 PM										
1:00 PM										
2:00 PM										
3:00 PM										
4:00 PM										
5:00 PM										
6:00 PM										
7:00 PM										
8:00 PM										
9:00 PM										
10:00 PM										
11:00 PM										
12:00 AM										
1:00 AM										
2:00 AM										
3:00 AM										
4:00 AM										

INSTRUCTIONS: Place a mark each hour to denote what your baby's main mood was over the previous hour. Place a mark at the estimated times of spit-ups, vomiting, feedings, or diaper changes. *Make additional notes below.*

DAILY LOG RECORD

Date: _____ Day of the Week: _____

What I'm grateful for today:

How I'm going to care for/reward myself today:

How am I feeling today?

Current food trials (if any):

Number of days my baby or I have been avoiding this food:

DAILY LOG CHART SUMMARY

(fill this out after today's chart on the next page is complete)

Total estimated crying time today:
Any concerns?

Total estimated sleeping time:
Any concerns?

Total number of vomiting episodes:
Any concerns?

Daily Log Chart

	Feeding	Diaper change	Vomiting	Spit-up	Extreme Crying	Crying	Moderate fussiness	Mild fussiness	Content	Sleeping
5:00 AM										
6:00 AM										
7:00 AM										
8:00 AM										
9:00 AM										
10:00 AM										
11:00 AM										
12:00 PM										
1:00 PM										
2:00 PM										
3:00 PM										
4:00 PM										
5:00 PM										
6:00 PM										
7:00 PM										
8:00 PM										
9:00 PM										
10:00 PM										
11:00 PM										
12:00 AM										
1:00 AM										
2:00 AM										
3:00 AM										
4:00 AM										

INSTRUCTIONS: Place a mark each hour to denote what your baby's main mood was over the previous hour. Place a mark at the estimated times of spit-ups, vomiting, feedings, or diaper changes. *Make additional notes below.*

Daily Log Record

Date: _____   Day of the Week: _____

What I'm grateful for today:

How I'm going to care for/reward myself today:

How am I feeling today?

Current food trials (if any):

Number of days my baby or I have been avoiding this food:

Daily Log Chart Summary

(fill this out after today's chart on the next page is complete)

Total estimated crying time today:
Any concerns?

Total estimated sleeping time:
Any concerns?

Total number of vomiting episodes:
Any concerns?

DAILY LOG CHART

	Feeding	Diaper change	Vomiting	Spit-up	Extreme Crying	Crying	Moderate fussiness	Mild fussiness	Content	Sleeping
5:00 AM										
6:00 AM										
7:00 AM										
8:00 AM										
9:00 AM										
10:00 AM										
11:00 AM										
12:00 PM										
1:00 PM										
2:00 PM										
3:00 PM										
4:00 PM										
5:00 PM										
6:00 PM										
7:00 PM										
8:00 PM										
9:00 PM										
10:00 PM										
11:00 PM										
12:00 AM										
1:00 AM										
2:00 AM										
3:00 AM										
4:00 AM										

INSTRUCTIONS: Place a mark each hour to denote what your baby's main mood was over the previous hour. Place a mark at the estimated times of spit-ups, vomiting, feedings, or diaper changes. *Make additional notes below.*

"gratitude is not found by acknowledging what you should be thankful for, rather it lies in recognizing what truly brings you joy"

Weekly Summary Sheet

My baby's age (in weeks):

What was the highlight (best thing that happened) this week?

Observations of my baby's crying behavior this week (e.g., how many hours on average per day did my baby cry? What time of day? Did the crying seem to correlate with certain needs or events?)

Observations of my baby's feeding and digestive patterns this week (including latching, feeding, vomiting issues, etc.):

Notes/questions from this week to remember for my pediatrician or lactation specialist:

Any lessons I need to remember from this week? (e.g., what activities did my baby seem to enjoy most?)

What I'm going to ask for more help with next week:

WEEK THREE

DAILY LOG RECORD

Date: _____ Day of the Week: _____

What I'm grateful for today:

How I'm going to care for/reward myself today:

How am I feeling today?

Current food trials (if any):

Number of days my baby or I have been avoiding this food:

DAILY LOG CHART SUMMARY

(fill this out after today's chart on the next page is complete)

Total estimated crying time today:
Any concerns?

Total estimated sleeping time:
Any concerns?

Total number of vomiting episodes:
Any concerns?

Daily Log Chart

	Feeding	Diaper change	Vomiting	Spit-up	Extreme Crying	Crying	Moderate fussiness	Mild fussiness	Content	Sleeping
5:00 AM										
6:00 AM										
7:00 AM										
8:00 AM										
9:00 AM										
10:00 AM										
11:00 AM										
12:00 PM										
1:00 PM										
2:00 PM										
3:00 PM										
4:00 PM										
5:00 PM										
6:00 PM										
7:00 PM										
8:00 PM										
9:00 PM										
10:00 PM										
11:00 PM										
12:00 AM										
1:00 AM										
2:00 AM										
3:00 AM										
4:00 AM										

INSTRUCTIONS: Place a mark each hour to denote what your baby's main mood was over the previous hour. Place a mark at the estimated times of spit-ups, vomiting, feedings, or diaper changes. *Make additional notes below.*

DAILY LOG RECORD

Date: _____ Day of the Week: _____

What I'm grateful for today:

How I'm going to care for/reward myself today:

How am I feeling today?

Current food trials (if any):

Number of days my baby or I have been avoiding this food:

DAILY LOG CHART SUMMARY

(fill this out after today's chart on the next page is complete)

Total estimated crying time today:
Any concerns?

Total estimated sleeping time:
Any concerns?

Total number of vomiting episodes:
Any concerns?

DAILY LOG CHART

	Feeding	Diaper change	Vomiting	Spit-up	Extreme Crying	Crying	Moderate fussiness	Mild fussiness	Content	Sleeping
5:00 AM										
6:00 AM										
7:00 AM										
8:00 AM										
9:00 AM										
10:00 AM										
11:00 AM										
12:00 PM										
1:00 PM										
2:00 PM										
3:00 PM										
4:00 PM										
5:00 PM										
6:00 PM										
7:00 PM										
8:00 PM										
9:00 PM										
10:00 PM										
11:00 PM										
12:00 AM										
1:00 AM										
2:00 AM										
3:00 AM										
4:00 AM										

INSTRUCTIONS: Place a mark each hour to denote what your baby's main mood was over the previous hour. Place a mark at the estimated times of spit-ups, vomiting, feedings, or diaper changes. *Make additional notes below.*

DAILY LOG RECORD

Date: _____   Day of the Week: _____

What I'm grateful for today:

How I'm going to care for/reward myself today:

How am I feeling today?

Current food trials (if any):

Number of days my baby or I have been avoiding this food:

DAILY LOG CHART SUMMARY

(fill this out after today's chart on the next page is complete)

Total estimated crying time today:
Any concerns?

Total estimated sleeping time:
Any concerns?

Total number of vomiting episodes:
Any concerns?

Daily Log Chart

	Feeding	Diaper change	Vomiting	Spit-up	Extreme Crying	Crying	Moderate fussiness	Mild fussiness	Content	Sleeping
5:00 AM										
6:00 AM										
7:00 AM										
8:00 AM										
9:00 AM										
10:00 AM										
11:00 AM										
12:00 PM										
1:00 PM										
2:00 PM										
3:00 PM										
4:00 PM										
5:00 PM										
6:00 PM										
7:00 PM										
8:00 PM										
9:00 PM										
10:00 PM										
11:00 PM										
12:00 AM										
1:00 AM										
2:00 AM										
3:00 AM										
4:00 AM										

INSTRUCTIONS: Place a mark each hour to denote what your baby's main mood was over the previous hour. Place a mark at the estimated times of spit-ups, vomiting, feedings, or diaper changes. *Make additional notes below.*

Daily Log Record

Date: _____ Day of the Week: _____

What I'm grateful for today:

How I'm going to care for/reward myself today:

How am I feeling today?

Current food trials (if any):

Number of days my baby or I have been avoiding this food:

Daily Log Chart Summary

(fill this out after today's chart on the next page is complete)

Total estimated crying time today:
Any concerns?

Total estimated sleeping time:
Any concerns?

Total number of vomiting episodes:
Any concerns?

Daily Log Chart

	Feeding	Diaper change	Vomiting	Spit-up	Extreme Crying	Crying	Moderate fussiness	Mild fussiness	Content	Sleeping
5:00 AM										
6:00 AM										
7:00 AM										
8:00 AM										
9:00 AM										
10:00 AM										
11:00 AM										
12:00 PM										
1:00 PM										
2:00 PM										
3:00 PM										
4:00 PM										
5:00 PM										
6:00 PM										
7:00 PM										
8:00 PM										
9:00 PM										
10:00 PM										
11:00 PM										
12:00 AM										
1:00 AM										
2:00 AM										
3:00 AM										
4:00 AM										

INSTRUCTIONS: Place a mark each hour to denote what your baby's main mood was over the previous hour. Place a mark at the estimated times of spit-ups, vomiting, feedings, or diaper changes. *Make additional notes below.*

DAILY LOG RECORD

Date: _____   Day of the Week: _____

What I'm grateful for today:

How I'm going to care for/reward myself today:

How am I feeling today?

Current food trials (if any):

Number of days my baby or I have been avoiding this food:

DAILY LOG CHART SUMMARY

(fill this out after today's chart on the next page is complete)

Total estimated crying time today:
Any concerns?

Total estimated sleeping time:
Any concerns?

Total number of vomiting episodes:
Any concerns?

Daily Log Chart

	Feeding	Diaper change	Vomiting	Spit-up	Extreme Crying	Crying	Moderate fussiness	Mild fussiness	Content	Sleeping
5:00 AM										
6:00 AM										
7:00 AM										
8:00 AM										
9:00 AM										
10:00 AM										
11:00 AM										
12:00 PM										
1:00 PM										
2:00 PM										
3:00 PM										
4:00 PM										
5:00 PM										
6:00 PM										
7:00 PM										
8:00 PM										
9:00 PM										
10:00 PM										
11:00 PM										
12:00 AM										
1:00 AM										
2:00 AM										
3:00 AM										
4:00 AM										

INSTRUCTIONS: Place a mark each hour to denote what your baby's main mood was over the previous hour. Place a mark at the estimated times of spit-ups, vomiting, feedings, or diaper changes. *Make additional notes below.*

Daily Log Record

Date: _____   Day of the Week: _____

What I'm grateful for today:

How I'm going to care for/reward myself today:

How am I feeling today?

Current food trials (if any):

Number of days my baby or I have been avoiding this food:

Daily Log Chart Summary

(fill this out after today's chart on the next page is complete)

Total estimated crying time today:
Any concerns?

Total estimated sleeping time:
Any concerns?

Total number of vomiting episodes:
Any concerns?

Daily Log Chart

	Feeding	Diaper change	Vomiting	Spit-up	Extreme Crying	Crying	Moderate fussiness	Mild fussiness	Content	Sleeping
5:00 AM										
6:00 AM										
7:00 AM										
8:00 AM										
9:00 AM										
10:00 AM										
11:00 AM										
12:00 PM										
1:00 PM										
2:00 PM										
3:00 PM										
4:00 PM										
5:00 PM										
6:00 PM										
7:00 PM										
8:00 PM										
9:00 PM										
10:00 PM										
11:00 PM										
12:00 AM										
1:00 AM										
2:00 AM										
3:00 AM										
4:00 AM										

INSTRUCTIONS: Place a mark each hour to denote what your baby's main mood was over the previous hour. Place a mark at the estimated times of spit-ups, vomiting, feedings, or diaper changes. *Make additional notes below.*

Daily Log Record

Date: _____   Day of the Week: _____

What I'm grateful for today:

How I'm going to care for/reward myself today:

How am I feeling today?

Current food trials (if any):

Number of days my baby or I have been avoiding this food:

Daily Log Chart Summary

(fill this out after today's chart on the next page is complete)

Total estimated crying time today:
Any concerns?

Total estimated sleeping time:
Any concerns?

Total number of vomiting episodes:
Any concerns?

Daily Log Chart

	Feeding	Diaper change	Vomiting	Spit-up	Extreme Crying	Crying	Moderate fussiness	Mild fussiness	Content	Sleeping
5:00 AM										
6:00 AM										
7:00 AM										
8:00 AM										
9:00 AM										
10:00 AM										
11:00 AM										
12:00 PM										
1:00 PM										
2:00 PM										
3:00 PM										
4:00 PM										
5:00 PM										
6:00 PM										
7:00 PM										
8:00 PM										
9:00 PM										
10:00 PM										
11:00 PM										
12:00 AM										
1:00 AM										
2:00 AM										
3:00 AM										
4:00 AM										

INSTRUCTIONS: Place a mark each hour to denote what your baby's main mood was over the previous hour. Place a mark at the estimated times of spit-ups, vomiting, feedings, or diaper changes. *Make additional notes below.*

"enhance your ability to cope through self-compassion"

Weekly Summary Sheet

My baby's age (in weeks):

What was the highlight (best thing that happened) this week?

Observations of my baby's crying behavior this week (e.g., how many hours on average per day did my baby cry? What time of day? Did the crying seem to correlate with certain needs or events?)

Observations of my baby's feeding and digestive patterns this week (including latching, feeding, vomiting issues, etc.):

Notes/questions from this week to remember for my pediatrician or lactation specialist:

Any lessons I need to remember from this week? (e.g., what activities did my baby seem to enjoy most?)

What I'm going to ask for more help with next week:

WEEK FOUR

Daily Log Record

Date: _____   Day of the Week: _____

What I'm grateful for today:

How I'm going to care for/reward myself today:

How am I feeling today?

Current food trials (if any):

Number of days my baby or I have been avoiding this food:

Daily Log Chart Summary

(fill this out after today's chart on the next page is complete)

Total estimated crying time today:
Any concerns?

Total estimated sleeping time:
Any concerns?

Total number of vomiting episodes:
Any concerns?

DAILY LOG CHART

	Feeding	Diaper change	Vomiting	Spit-up	Extreme Crying	Crying	Moderate fussiness	Mild fussiness	Content	Sleeping
5:00 AM										
6:00 AM										
7:00 AM										
8:00 AM										
9:00 AM										
10:00 AM										
11:00 AM										
12:00 PM										
1:00 PM										
2:00 PM										
3:00 PM										
4:00 PM										
5:00 PM										
6:00 PM										
7:00 PM										
8:00 PM										
9:00 PM										
10:00 PM										
11:00 PM										
12:00 AM										
1:00 AM										
2:00 AM										
3:00 AM										
4:00 AM										

INSTRUCTIONS: Place a mark each hour to denote what your baby's main mood was over the previous hour. Place a mark at the estimated times of spit-ups, vomiting, feedings, or diaper changes. *Make additional notes below.*

Daily Log Record

Date: _____ Day of the Week: _____

What I'm grateful for today:

How I'm going to care for/reward myself today:

How am I feeling today?

Current food trials (if any):

Number of days my baby or I have been avoiding this food:

Daily Log Chart Summary

(fill this out after today's chart on the next page is complete)

Total estimated crying time today:
Any concerns?

Total estimated sleeping time:
Any concerns?

Total number of vomiting episodes:
Any concerns?

Daily Log Chart

	Feeding	Diaper change	Vomiting	Spit-up	Extreme Crying	Crying	Moderate fussiness	Mild fussiness	Content	Sleeping
5:00 AM										
6:00 AM										
7:00 AM										
8:00 AM										
9:00 AM										
10:00 AM										
11:00 AM										
12:00 PM										
1:00 PM										
2:00 PM										
3:00 PM										
4:00 PM										
5:00 PM										
6:00 PM										
7:00 PM										
8:00 PM										
9:00 PM										
10:00 PM										
11:00 PM										
12:00 AM										
1:00 AM										
2:00 AM										
3:00 AM										
4:00 AM										

INSTRUCTIONS: Place a mark each hour to denote what your baby's main mood was over the previous hour. Place a mark at the estimated times of spit-ups, vomiting, feedings, or diaper changes. *Make additional notes below.*

DAILY LOG RECORD

Date: _____ Day of the Week: _____

What I'm grateful for today:

How I'm going to care for/reward myself today:

How am I feeling today?

Current food trials (if any):

Number of days my baby or I have been avoiding this food:

DAILY LOG CHART SUMMARY

(fill this out after today's chart on the next page is complete)

Total estimated crying time today:
Any concerns?

Total estimated sleeping time:
Any concerns?

Total number of vomiting episodes:
Any concerns?

Daily Log Chart

	Feeding	Diaper change	Vomiting	Spit-up	Extreme Crying	Crying	Moderate fussiness	Mild fussiness	Content	Sleeping
5:00 AM										
6:00 AM										
7:00 AM										
8:00 AM										
9:00 AM										
10:00 AM										
11:00 AM										
12:00 PM										
1:00 PM										
2:00 PM										
3:00 PM										
4:00 PM										
5:00 PM										
6:00 PM										
7:00 PM										
8:00 PM										
9:00 PM										
10:00 PM										
11:00 PM										
12:00 AM										
1:00 AM										
2:00 AM										
3:00 AM										
4:00 AM										

INSTRUCTIONS: Place a mark each hour to denote what your baby's main mood was over the previous hour. Place a mark at the estimated times of spit-ups, vomiting, feedings, or diaper changes. *Make additional notes below.*

Daily Log Record

Date: _____ Day of the Week: _____

What I'm grateful for today:

How I'm going to care for/reward myself today:

How am I feeling today?

Current food trials (if any):

Number of days my baby or I have been avoiding this food:

Daily Log Chart Summary

(fill this out after today's chart on the next page is complete)

Total estimated crying time today:
Any concerns?

Total estimated sleeping time:
Any concerns?

Total number of vomiting episodes:
Any concerns?

Daily Log Chart

	Feeding	Diaper change	Vomiting	Spit-up	Extreme Crying	Crying	Moderate fussiness	Mild fussiness	Content	Sleeping
5:00 AM										
6:00 AM										
7:00 AM										
8:00 AM										
9:00 AM										
10:00 AM										
11:00 AM										
12:00 PM										
1:00 PM										
2:00 PM										
3:00 PM										
4:00 PM										
5:00 PM										
6:00 PM										
7:00 PM										
8:00 PM										
9:00 PM										
10:00 PM										
11:00 PM										
12:00 AM										
1:00 AM										
2:00 AM										
3:00 AM										
4:00 AM										

INSTRUCTIONS: Place a mark each hour to denote what your baby's main mood was over the previous hour. Place a mark at the estimated times of spit-ups, vomiting, feedings, or diaper changes. *Make additional notes below.*

DAILY LOG RECORD

Date: _____ Day of the Week: _____

What I'm grateful for today:

How I'm going to care for/reward myself today:

How am I feeling today?

Current food trials (if any):

Number of days my baby or I have been avoiding this food:

DAILY LOG CHART SUMMARY

(fill this out after today's chart on the next page is complete)

Total estimated crying time today:
Any concerns?

Total estimated sleeping time:
Any concerns?

Total number of vomiting episodes:
Any concerns?

DAILY LOG CHART

	Feeding	Diaper change	Vomiting	Spit-up	Extreme Crying	Crying	Moderate fussiness	Mild fussiness	Content	Sleeping
5:00 AM										
6:00 AM										
7:00 AM										
8:00 AM										
9:00 AM										
10:00 AM										
11:00 AM										
12:00 PM										
1:00 PM										
2:00 PM										
3:00 PM										
4:00 PM										
5:00 PM										
6:00 PM										
7:00 PM										
8:00 PM										
9:00 PM										
10:00 PM										
11:00 PM										
12:00 AM										
1:00 AM										
2:00 AM										
3:00 AM										
4:00 AM										

INSTRUCTIONS: Place a mark each hour to denote what your baby's main mood was over the previous hour. Place a mark at the estimated times of spit-ups, vomiting, feedings, or diaper changes. *Make additional notes below.*

Daily Log Record

Date: _____ Day of the Week: _____

What I'm grateful for today:

How I'm going to care for/reward myself today:

How am I feeling today?

Current food trials (if any):

Number of days my baby or I have been avoiding this food:

Daily Log Chart Summary

(fill this out after today's chart on the next page is complete)

Total estimated crying time today:
Any concerns?

Total estimated sleeping time:
Any concerns?

Total number of vomiting episodes:
Any concerns?

Daily Log Chart

	Feeding	Diaper change	Vomiting	Spit-up	Extreme Crying	Crying	Moderate fussiness	Mild fussiness	Content	Sleeping
5:00 AM										
6:00 AM										
7:00 AM										
8:00 AM										
9:00 AM										
10:00 AM										
11:00 AM										
12:00 PM										
1:00 PM										
2:00 PM										
3:00 PM										
4:00 PM										
5:00 PM										
6:00 PM										
7:00 PM										
8:00 PM										
9:00 PM										
10:00 PM										
11:00 PM										
12:00 AM										
1:00 AM										
2:00 AM										
3:00 AM										
4:00 AM										

INSTRUCTIONS: Place a mark each hour to denote what your baby's main mood was over the previous hour. Place a mark at the estimated times of spit-ups, vomiting, feedings, or diaper changes. *Make additional notes below.*

Daily Log Record

Date: _____ Day of the Week: _____

What I'm grateful for today:

How I'm going to care for/reward myself today:

How am I feeling today?

Current food trials (if any):

Number of days my baby or I have been avoiding this food:

Daily Log Chart Summary

(fill this out after today's chart on the next page is complete)

Total estimated crying time today:
Any concerns?

Total estimated sleeping time:
Any concerns?

Total number of vomiting episodes:
Any concerns?

Daily Log Chart

	Feeding	Diaper change	Vomiting	Spit-up	Extreme Crying	Crying	Moderate fussiness	Mild fussiness	Content	Sleeping
5:00 AM										
6:00 AM										
7:00 AM										
8:00 AM										
9:00 AM										
10:00 AM										
11:00 AM										
12:00 PM										
1:00 PM										
2:00 PM										
3:00 PM										
4:00 PM										
5:00 PM										
6:00 PM										
7:00 PM										
8:00 PM										
9:00 PM										
10:00 PM										
11:00 PM										
12:00 AM										
1:00 AM										
2:00 AM										
3:00 AM										
4:00 AM										

INSTRUCTIONS: Place a mark each hour to denote what your baby's main mood was over the previous hour. Place a mark at the estimated times of spit-ups, vomiting, feedings, or diaper changes. *Make additional notes below.*

"empathy requires less judgement
and more honesty"

Weekly Summary Sheet

My baby's age (in weeks):

What was the highlight (best thing that happened) this week?

Observations of my baby's crying behavior this week (e.g., how many hours on average per day did my baby cry? What time of day? Did the crying seem to correlate with certain needs or events?)

Observations of my baby's feeding and digestive patterns this week (including latching, feeding, vomiting issues, etc.):

Notes/questions from this week to remember for my pediatrician or lactation specialist:

Any lessons I need to remember from this week? (e.g., what activities did my baby seem to enjoy most?)

What I'm going to ask for more help with next week:

WEEK FIVE

Daily Log Record

Date: _____   Day of the Week: _____

What I'm grateful for today:

How I'm going to care for/reward myself today:

How am I feeling today?

Current food trials (if any):

Number of days my baby or I have been avoiding this food:

Daily Log Chart Summary

(fill this out after today's chart on the next page is complete)

Total estimated crying time today:
Any concerns?

Total estimated sleeping time:
Any concerns?

Total number of vomiting episodes:
Any concerns?

DAILY LOG CHART

	Feeding	Diaper change	Vomiting	Spit-up	Extreme Crying	Crying	Moderate fussiness	Mild fussiness	Content	Sleeping
5:00 AM										
6:00 AM										
7:00 AM										
8:00 AM										
9:00 AM										
10:00 AM										
11:00 AM										
12:00 PM										
1:00 PM										
2:00 PM										
3:00 PM										
4:00 PM										
5:00 PM										
6:00 PM										
7:00 PM										
8:00 PM										
9:00 PM										
10:00 PM										
11:00 PM										
12:00 AM										
1:00 AM										
2:00 AM										
3:00 AM										
4:00 AM										

INSTRUCTIONS: Place a mark each hour to denote what your baby's main mood was over the previous hour. Place a mark at the estimated times of spit-ups, vomiting, feedings, or diaper changes. *Make additional notes below.*

Daily Log Record

Date: _____ Day of the Week: _____

What I'm grateful for today:

How I'm going to care for/reward myself today:

How am I feeling today?

Current food trials (if any):

Number of days my baby or I have been avoiding this food:

Daily Log Chart Summary

(fill this out after today's chart on the next page is complete)

Total estimated crying time today:
Any concerns?

Total estimated sleeping time:
Any concerns?

Total number of vomiting episodes:
Any concerns?

Daily Log Chart

	Feeding	Diaper change	Vomiting	Spit-up	Extreme Crying	Crying	Moderate fussiness	Mild fussiness	Content	Sleeping
5:00 AM										
6:00 AM										
7:00 AM										
8:00 AM										
9:00 AM										
10:00 AM										
11:00 AM										
12:00 PM										
1:00 PM										
2:00 PM										
3:00 PM										
4:00 PM										
5:00 PM										
6:00 PM										
7:00 PM										
8:00 PM										
9:00 PM										
10:00 PM										
11:00 PM										
12:00 AM										
1:00 AM										
2:00 AM										
3:00 AM										
4:00 AM										

INSTRUCTIONS: Place a mark each hour to denote what your baby's main mood was over the previous hour. Place a mark at the estimated times of spit-ups, vomiting, feedings, or diaper changes. *Make additional notes below.*

Daily Log Record

Date: _____ Day of the Week: _____

What I'm grateful for today:

How I'm going to care for/reward myself today:

How am I feeling today?

Current food trials (if any):

Number of days my baby or I have been avoiding this food:

Daily Log Chart Summary

(fill this out after today's chart on the next page is complete)

Total estimated crying time today:
Any concerns?

Total estimated sleeping time:
Any concerns?

Total number of vomiting episodes:
Any concerns?

Daily Log Chart

	Feeding	Diaper change	Vomiting	Spit-up	Extreme Crying	Crying	Moderate fussiness	Mild fussiness	Content	Sleeping
5:00 AM										
6:00 AM										
7:00 AM										
8:00 AM										
9:00 AM										
10:00 AM										
11:00 AM										
12:00 PM										
1:00 PM										
2:00 PM										
3:00 PM										
4:00 PM										
5:00 PM										
6:00 PM										
7:00 PM										
8:00 PM										
9:00 PM										
10:00 PM										
11:00 PM										
12:00 AM										
1:00 AM										
2:00 AM										
3:00 AM										
4:00 AM										

INSTRUCTIONS: Place a mark each hour to denote what your baby's main mood was over the previous hour. Place a mark at the estimated times of spit-ups, vomiting, feedings, or diaper changes. *Make additional notes below.*

DAILY LOG RECORD

Date: _____   Day of the Week: _____

What I'm grateful for today:

How I'm going to care for/reward myself today:

How am I feeling today?

Current food trials (if any):

Number of days my baby or I have been avoiding this food:

DAILY LOG CHART SUMMARY

(fill this out after today's chart on the next page is complete)

Total estimated crying time today:
Any concerns?

Total estimated sleeping time:
Any concerns?

Total number of vomiting episodes:
Any concerns?

Daily Log Chart

	Feeding	Diaper change	Vomiting	Spit-up	Extreme Crying	Crying	Moderate fussiness	Mild fussiness	Content	Sleeping
5:00 AM										
6:00 AM										
7:00 AM										
8:00 AM										
9:00 AM										
10:00 AM										
11:00 AM										
12:00 PM										
1:00 PM										
2:00 PM										
3:00 PM										
4:00 PM										
5:00 PM										
6:00 PM										
7:00 PM										
8:00 PM										
9:00 PM										
10:00 PM										
11:00 PM										
12:00 AM										
1:00 AM										
2:00 AM										
3:00 AM										
4:00 AM										

INSTRUCTIONS: Place a mark each hour to denote what your baby's main mood was over the previous hour. Place a mark at the estimated times of spit-ups, vomiting, feedings, or diaper changes. *Make additional notes below.*

Daily Log Record

Date: _____   Day of the Week: _____

What I'm grateful for today:

How I'm going to care for/reward myself today:

How am I feeling today?

Current food trials (if any):

Number of days my baby or I have been avoiding this food:

Daily Log Chart Summary

(fill this out after today's chart on the next page is complete)

Total estimated crying time today:
Any concerns?

Total estimated sleeping time:
Any concerns?

Total number of vomiting episodes:
Any concerns?

DAILY LOG CHART

	Feeding	Diaper change	Vomiting	Spit-up	Extreme Crying	Crying	Moderate fussiness	Mild fussiness	Content	Sleeping
5:00 AM										
6:00 AM										
7:00 AM										
8:00 AM										
9:00 AM										
10:00 AM										
11:00 AM										
12:00 PM										
1:00 PM										
2:00 PM										
3:00 PM										
4:00 PM										
5:00 PM										
6:00 PM										
7:00 PM										
8:00 PM										
9:00 PM										
10:00 PM										
11:00 PM										
12:00 AM										
1:00 AM										
2:00 AM										
3:00 AM										
4:00 AM										

INSTRUCTIONS: Place a mark each hour to denote what your baby's main mood was over the previous hour. Place a mark at the estimated times of spit-ups, vomiting, feedings, or diaper changes. *Make additional notes below.*

Daily Log Record

Date: _____ Day of the Week: _____

What I'm grateful for today:

How I'm going to care for/reward myself today:

How am I feeling today?

Current food trials (if any):

Number of days my baby or I have been avoiding this food:

Daily Log Chart Summary

(fill this out after today's chart on the next page is complete)

Total estimated crying time today:
Any concerns?

Total estimated sleeping time:
Any concerns?

Total number of vomiting episodes:
Any concerns?

Daily Log Chart

	Feeding	Diaper change	Vomiting	Spit-up	Extreme Crying	Crying	Moderate fussiness	Mild fussiness	Content	Sleeping
5:00 AM										
6:00 AM										
7:00 AM										
8:00 AM										
9:00 AM										
10:00 AM										
11:00 AM										
12:00 PM										
1:00 PM										
2:00 PM										
3:00 PM										
4:00 PM										
5:00 PM										
6:00 PM										
7:00 PM										
8:00 PM										
9:00 PM										
10:00 PM										
11:00 PM										
12:00 AM										
1:00 AM										
2:00 AM										
3:00 AM										
4:00 AM										

INSTRUCTIONS: Place a mark each hour to denote what your baby's main mood was over the previous hour. Place a mark at the estimated times of spit-ups, vomiting, feedings, or diaper changes. *Make additional notes below.*

Daily Log Record

Date: _____   Day of the Week: _____

What I'm grateful for today:

How I'm going to care for/reward myself today:

How am I feeling today?

Current food trials (if any):

Number of days my baby or I have been avoiding this food:

Daily Log Chart Summary

(fill this out after today's chart on the next page is complete)

Total estimated crying time today:
Any concerns?

Total estimated sleeping time:
Any concerns?

Total number of vomiting episodes:
Any concerns?

Daily Log Chart

	Feeding	Diaper change	Vomiting	Spit-up	Extreme Crying	Crying	Moderate fussiness	Mild fussiness	Content	Sleeping
5:00 AM										
6:00 AM										
7:00 AM										
8:00 AM										
9:00 AM										
10:00 AM										
11:00 AM										
12:00 PM										
1:00 PM										
2:00 PM										
3:00 PM										
4:00 PM										
5:00 PM										
6:00 PM										
7:00 PM										
8:00 PM										
9:00 PM										
10:00 PM										
11:00 PM										
12:00 AM										
1:00 AM										
2:00 AM										
3:00 AM										
4:00 AM										

INSTRUCTIONS: Place a mark each hour to denote what your baby's main mood was over the previous hour. Place a mark at the estimated times of spit-ups, vomiting, feedings, or diaper changes. *Make additional notes below.*

"when you feel like crying,
try laughing instead"

WEEKLY SUMMARY SHEET

My baby's age (in weeks):

What was the highlight (best thing that happened) this week?

Observations of my baby's crying behavior this week (e.g., how many hours on average per day did my baby cry? What time of day? Did the crying seem to correlate with certain needs or events?)

Observations of my baby's feeding and digestive patterns this week (including latching, feeding, vomiting issues, etc.):

Notes/questions from this week to remember for my pediatrician or lactation specialist:

Any lessons I need to remember from this week? (e.g., what activities did my baby seem to enjoy most?)

What I'm going to ask for more help with next week:

WEEK SIX

Daily Log Record

Date: _____ Day of the Week: _____

What I'm grateful for today:

How I'm going to care for/reward myself today:

How am I feeling today?

Current food trials (if any):

Number of days my baby or I have been avoiding this food:

Daily Log Chart Summary

(fill this out after today's chart on the next page is complete)

Total estimated crying time today:
Any concerns?

Total estimated sleeping time:
Any concerns?

Total number of vomiting episodes:
Any concerns?

Daily Log Chart

	Feeding	Diaper change	Vomiting	Spit-up	Extreme Crying	Crying	Moderate fussiness	Mild fussiness	Content	Sleeping
5:00 AM										
6:00 AM										
7:00 AM										
8:00 AM										
9:00 AM										
10:00 AM										
11:00 AM										
12:00 PM										
1:00 PM										
2:00 PM										
3:00 PM										
4:00 PM										
5:00 PM										
6:00 PM										
7:00 PM										
8:00 PM										
9:00 PM										
10:00 PM										
11:00 PM										
12:00 AM										
1:00 AM										
2:00 AM										
3:00 AM										
4:00 AM										

INSTRUCTIONS: Place a mark each hour to denote what your baby's main mood was over the previous hour. Place a mark at the estimated times of spit-ups, vomiting, feedings, or diaper changes. *Make additional notes below.*

Daily Log Record

Date: _____   Day of the Week: _____

What I'm grateful for today:

How I'm going to care for/reward myself today:

How am I feeling today?

Current food trials (if any):

Number of days my baby or I have been avoiding this food:

Daily Log Chart Summary

(fill this out after today's chart on the next page is complete)

Total estimated crying time today:
Any concerns?

Total estimated sleeping time:
Any concerns?

Total number of vomiting episodes:
Any concerns?

Daily Log Chart

	Feeding	Diaper change	Vomiting	Spit-up	Extreme Crying	Crying	Moderate fussiness	Mild fussiness	Content	Sleeping
5:00 AM										
6:00 AM										
7:00 AM										
8:00 AM										
9:00 AM										
10:00 AM										
11:00 AM										
12:00 PM										
1:00 PM										
2:00 PM										
3:00 PM										
4:00 PM										
5:00 PM										
6:00 PM										
7:00 PM										
8:00 PM										
9:00 PM										
10:00 PM										
11:00 PM										
12:00 AM										
1:00 AM										
2:00 AM										
3:00 AM										
4:00 AM										

INSTRUCTIONS: Place a mark each hour to denote what your baby's main mood was over the previous hour. Place a mark at the estimated times of spit-ups, vomiting, feedings, or diaper changes. *Make additional notes below.*

Daily Log Record

Date: _____   Day of the Week: _____

What I'm grateful for today:

How I'm going to care for/reward myself today:

How am I feeling today?

Current food trials (if any):

Number of days my baby or I have been avoiding this food:

Daily Log Chart Summary

(fill this out after today's chart on the next page is complete)

Total estimated crying time today:
Any concerns?

Total estimated sleeping time:
Any concerns?

Total number of vomiting episodes:
Any concerns?

Daily Log Chart

	Feeding	Diaper change	Vomiting	Spit-up	Extreme Crying	Crying	Moderate fussiness	Mild fussiness	Content	Sleeping
5:00 AM										
6:00 AM										
7:00 AM										
8:00 AM										
9:00 AM										
10:00 AM										
11:00 AM										
12:00 PM										
1:00 PM										
2:00 PM										
3:00 PM										
4:00 PM										
5:00 PM										
6:00 PM										
7:00 PM										
8:00 PM										
9:00 PM										
10:00 PM										
11:00 PM										
12:00 AM										
1:00 AM										
2:00 AM										
3:00 AM										
4:00 AM										

INSTRUCTIONS: Place a mark each hour to denote what your baby's main mood was over the previous hour. Place a mark at the estimated times of spit-ups, vomiting, feedings, or diaper changes. *Make additional notes below.*

DAILY LOG RECORD

Date: _____   Day of the Week: _____

What I'm grateful for today:

How I'm going to care for/reward myself today:

How am I feeling today?

Current food trials (if any):

Number of days my baby or I have been avoiding this food:

DAILY LOG CHART SUMMARY

(fill this out after today's chart on the next page is complete)

Total estimated crying time today:
Any concerns?

Total estimated sleeping time:
Any concerns?

Total number of vomiting episodes:
Any concerns?

Daily Log Chart

	Feeding	Diaper change	Vomiting	Spit-up	Extreme Crying	Crying	Moderate fussiness	Mild fussiness	Content	Sleeping
5:00 AM										
6:00 AM										
7:00 AM										
8:00 AM										
9:00 AM										
10:00 AM										
11:00 AM										
12:00 PM										
1:00 PM										
2:00 PM										
3:00 PM										
4:00 PM										
5:00 PM										
6:00 PM										
7:00 PM										
8:00 PM										
9:00 PM										
10:00 PM										
11:00 PM										
12:00 AM										
1:00 AM										
2:00 AM										
3:00 AM										
4:00 AM										

INSTRUCTIONS: Place a mark each hour to denote what your baby's main mood was over the previous hour. Place a mark at the estimated times of spit-ups, vomiting, feedings, or diaper changes. *Make additional notes below.*

Daily Log Record

Date: _____ Day of the Week: _____

What I'm grateful for today:

How I'm going to care for/reward myself today:

How am I feeling today?

Current food trials (if any):

Number of days my baby or I have been avoiding this food:

Daily Log Chart Summary

(fill this out after today's chart on the next page is complete)

Total estimated crying time today:
Any concerns?

Total estimated sleeping time:
Any concerns?

Total number of vomiting episodes:
Any concerns?

Daily Log Chart

	Feeding	Diaper change	Vomiting	Spit-up	Extreme Crying	Crying	Moderate fussiness	Mild fussiness	Content	Sleeping
5:00 AM										
6:00 AM										
7:00 AM										
8:00 AM										
9:00 AM										
10:00 AM										
11:00 AM										
12:00 PM										
1:00 PM										
2:00 PM										
3:00 PM										
4:00 PM										
5:00 PM										
6:00 PM										
7:00 PM										
8:00 PM										
9:00 PM										
10:00 PM										
11:00 PM										
12:00 AM										
1:00 AM										
2:00 AM										
3:00 AM										
4:00 AM										

INSTRUCTIONS: Place a mark each hour to denote what your baby's main mood was over the previous hour. Place a mark at the estimated times of spit-ups, vomiting, feedings, or diaper changes. *Make additional notes below.*

Daily Log Record

Date: _____ Day of the Week: _____

What I'm grateful for today:

How I'm going to care for/reward myself today:

How am I feeling today?

Current food trials (if any):

Number of days my baby or I have been avoiding this food:

Daily Log Chart Summary

(fill this out after today's chart on the next page is complete)

Total estimated crying time today:
Any concerns?

Total estimated sleeping time:
Any concerns?

Total number of vomiting episodes:
Any concerns?

DAILY LOG CHART

	Feeding	Diaper change	Vomiting	Spit-up	Extreme Crying	Crying	Moderate fussiness	Mild fussiness	Content	Sleeping
5:00 AM										
6:00 AM										
7:00 AM										
8:00 AM										
9:00 AM										
10:00 AM										
11:00 AM										
12:00 PM										
1:00 PM										
2:00 PM										
3:00 PM										
4:00 PM										
5:00 PM										
6:00 PM										
7:00 PM										
8:00 PM										
9:00 PM										
10:00 PM										
11:00 PM										
12:00 AM										
1:00 AM										
2:00 AM										
3:00 AM										
4:00 AM										

INSTRUCTIONS: Place a mark each hour to denote what your baby's main mood was over the previous hour. Place a mark at the estimated times of spit-ups, vomiting, feedings, or diaper changes. *Make additional notes below.*

Daily Log Record

Date: _____ Day of the Week: _____

What I'm grateful for today:

How I'm going to care for/reward myself today:

How am I feeling today?

Current food trials (if any):

Number of days my baby or I have been avoiding this food:

Daily Log Chart Summary

(fill this out after today's chart on the next page is complete)

Total estimated crying time today:
Any concerns?

Total estimated sleeping time:
Any concerns?

Total number of vomiting episodes:
Any concerns?

DAILY LOG CHART

	Feeding	Diaper change	Vomiting	Spit-up	Extreme Crying	Crying	Moderate fussiness	Mild fussiness	Content	Sleeping
5:00 AM										
6:00 AM										
7:00 AM										
8:00 AM										
9:00 AM										
10:00 AM										
11:00 AM										
12:00 PM										
1:00 PM										
2:00 PM										
3:00 PM										
4:00 PM										
5:00 PM										
6:00 PM										
7:00 PM										
8:00 PM										
9:00 PM										
10:00 PM										
11:00 PM										
12:00 AM										
1:00 AM										
2:00 AM										
3:00 AM										
4:00 AM										

INSTRUCTIONS: Place a mark each hour to denote what your baby's main mood was over the previous hour. Place a mark at the estimated times of spit-ups, vomiting, feedings, or diaper changes. *Make additional notes below.*

"be a mother after your own heart"

Weekly Summary Sheet

My baby's age (in weeks):

What was the highlight (best thing that happened) this week?

Observations of my baby's crying behavior this week (e.g., how many hours on average per day did my baby cry? What time of day? Did the crying seem to correlate with certain needs or events?)

Observations of my baby's feeding and digestive patterns this week (including latching, feeding, vomiting issues, etc.):

Notes/questions from this week to remember for my pediatrician or lactation specialist:

Any lessons I need to remember from this week? (e.g., what activities did my baby seem to enjoy most?)

What I'm going to ask for more help with next week:

WEEK SEVEN

DAILY LOG RECORD

Date: _____   Day of the Week: _____

What I'm grateful for today:

How I'm going to care for/reward myself today:

How am I feeling today?

Current food trials (if any):

Number of days my baby or I have been avoiding this food:

DAILY LOG CHART SUMMARY

(fill this out after today's chart on the next page is complete)

Total estimated crying time today:
Any concerns?

Total estimated sleeping time:
Any concerns?

Total number of vomiting episodes:
Any concerns?

Daily Log Chart

	Feeding	Diaper change	Vomiting	Spit-up	Extreme Crying	Crying	Moderate fussiness	Mild fussiness	Content	Sleeping
5:00 AM										
6:00 AM										
7:00 AM										
8:00 AM										
9:00 AM										
10:00 AM										
11:00 AM										
12:00 PM										
1:00 PM										
2:00 PM										
3:00 PM										
4:00 PM										
5:00 PM										
6:00 PM										
7:00 PM										
8:00 PM										
9:00 PM										
10:00 PM										
11:00 PM										
12:00 AM										
1:00 AM										
2:00 AM										
3:00 AM										
4:00 AM										

INSTRUCTIONS: Place a mark each hour to denote what your baby's main mood was over the previous hour. Place a mark at the estimated times of spit-ups, vomiting, feedings, or diaper changes. *Make additional notes below.*

Daily Log Record

Date: _____ Day of the Week: _____

What I'm grateful for today:

How I'm going to care for/reward myself today:

How am I feeling today?

Current food trials (if any):

Number of days my baby or I have been avoiding this food:

Daily Log Chart Summary

(fill this out after today's chart on the next page is complete)

Total estimated crying time today:
Any concerns?

Total estimated sleeping time:
Any concerns?

Total number of vomiting episodes:
Any concerns?

Daily Log Chart

	Feeding	Diaper change	Vomiting	Spit-up	Extreme Crying	Crying	Moderate fussiness	Mild fussiness	Content	Sleeping
5:00 AM										
6:00 AM										
7:00 AM										
8:00 AM										
9:00 AM										
10:00 AM										
11:00 AM										
12:00 PM										
1:00 PM										
2:00 PM										
3:00 PM										
4:00 PM										
5:00 PM										
6:00 PM										
7:00 PM										
8:00 PM										
9:00 PM										
10:00 PM										
11:00 PM										
12:00 AM										
1:00 AM										
2:00 AM										
3:00 AM										
4:00 AM										

INSTRUCTIONS: Place a mark each hour to denote what your baby's main mood was over the previous hour. Place a mark at the estimated times of spit-ups, vomiting, feedings, or diaper changes. *Make additional notes below.*

DAILY LOG RECORD

Date: _____ Day of the Week: _____

What I'm grateful for today:

How I'm going to care for/reward myself today:

How am I feeling today?

Current food trials (if any):

Number of days my baby or I have been avoiding this food:

DAILY LOG CHART SUMMARY

(fill this out after today's chart on the next page is complete)

Total estimated crying time today:
Any concerns?

Total estimated sleeping time:
Any concerns?

Total number of vomiting episodes:
Any concerns?

Daily Log Chart

	Feeding	Diaper change	Vomiting	Spit-up	Extreme Crying	Crying	Moderate fussiness	Mild fussiness	Content	Sleeping
5:00 AM										
6:00 AM										
7:00 AM										
8:00 AM										
9:00 AM										
10:00 AM										
11:00 AM										
12:00 PM										
1:00 PM										
2:00 PM										
3:00 PM										
4:00 PM										
5:00 PM										
6:00 PM										
7:00 PM										
8:00 PM										
9:00 PM										
10:00 PM										
11:00 PM										
12:00 AM										
1:00 AM										
2:00 AM										
3:00 AM										
4:00 AM										

INSTRUCTIONS: Place a mark each hour to denote what your baby's main mood was over the previous hour. Place a mark at the estimated times of spit-ups, vomiting, feedings, or diaper changes. *Make additional notes below.*

DAILY LOG RECORD

Date: _____ Day of the Week: _____

What I'm grateful for today:

How I'm going to care for/reward myself today:

How am I feeling today?

Current food trials (if any):

Number of days my baby or I have been avoiding this food:

DAILY LOG CHART SUMMARY

(fill this out after today's chart on the next page is complete)

Total estimated crying time today:
Any concerns?

Total estimated sleeping time:
Any concerns?

Total number of vomiting episodes:
Any concerns?

Daily Log Chart

	Feeding	Diaper change	Vomiting	Spit-up	Extreme Crying	Crying	Moderate fussiness	Mild fussiness	Content	Sleeping
5:00 AM										
6:00 AM										
7:00 AM										
8:00 AM										
9:00 AM										
10:00 AM										
11:00 AM										
12:00 PM										
1:00 PM										
2:00 PM										
3:00 PM										
4:00 PM										
5:00 PM										
6:00 PM										
7:00 PM										
8:00 PM										
9:00 PM										
10:00 PM										
11:00 PM										
12:00 AM										
1:00 AM										
2:00 AM										
3:00 AM										
4:00 AM										

INSTRUCTIONS: Place a mark each hour to denote what your baby's main mood was over the previous hour. Place a mark at the estimated times of spit-ups, vomiting, feedings, or diaper changes. *Make additional notes below.*

DAILY LOG RECORD

Date: _____ Day of the Week: _____

What I'm grateful for today:

How I'm going to care for/reward myself today:

How am I feeling today?

Current food trials (if any):

Number of days my baby or I have been avoiding this food:

DAILY LOG CHART SUMMARY

(fill this out after today's chart on the next page is complete)

Total estimated crying time today:
Any concerns?

Total estimated sleeping time:
Any concerns?

Total number of vomiting episodes:
Any concerns?

DAILY LOG CHART

	Feeding	Diaper change	Vomiting	Spit-up	Extreme Crying	Crying	Moderate fussiness	Mild fussiness	Content	Sleeping
5:00 AM										
6:00 AM										
7:00 AM										
8:00 AM										
9:00 AM										
10:00 AM										
11:00 AM										
12:00 PM										
1:00 PM										
2:00 PM										
3:00 PM										
4:00 PM										
5:00 PM										
6:00 PM										
7:00 PM										
8:00 PM										
9:00 PM										
10:00 PM										
11:00 PM										
12:00 AM										
1:00 AM										
2:00 AM										
3:00 AM										
4:00 AM										

INSTRUCTIONS: Place a mark each hour to denote what your baby's main mood was over the previous hour. Place a mark at the estimated times of spit-ups, vomiting, feedings, or diaper changes. *Make additional notes below.*

Daily Log Record

Date: _____   Day of the Week: _____

What I'm grateful for today:

How I'm going to care for/reward myself today:

How am I feeling today?

Current food trials (if any):

Number of days my baby or I have been avoiding this food:

Daily Log Chart Summary

(fill this out after today's chart on the next page is complete)

Total estimated crying time today:
Any concerns?

Total estimated sleeping time:
Any concerns?

Total number of vomiting episodes:
Any concerns?

Daily Log Chart

	Feeding	Diaper change	Vomiting	Spit-up	Extreme Crying	Crying	Moderate fussiness	Mild fussiness	Content	Sleeping
5:00 AM										
6:00 AM										
7:00 AM										
8:00 AM										
9:00 AM										
10:00 AM										
11:00 AM										
12:00 PM										
1:00 PM										
2:00 PM										
3:00 PM										
4:00 PM										
5:00 PM										
6:00 PM										
7:00 PM										
8:00 PM										
9:00 PM										
10:00 PM										
11:00 PM										
12:00 AM										
1:00 AM										
2:00 AM										
3:00 AM										
4:00 AM										

INSTRUCTIONS: Place a mark each hour to denote what your baby's main mood was over the previous hour. Place a mark at the estimated times of spit-ups, vomiting, feedings, or diaper changes. *Make additional notes below.*

Daily Log Record

Date: _____   Day of the Week: _____

What I'm grateful for today:

How I'm going to care for/reward myself today:

How am I feeling today?

Current food trials (if any):

Number of days my baby or I have been avoiding this food:

Daily Log Chart Summary

(fill this out after today's chart on the next page is complete)

Total estimated crying time today:
Any concerns?

Total estimated sleeping time:
Any concerns?

Total number of vomiting episodes:
Any concerns?

DAILY LOG CHART

	Feeding	Diaper change	Vomiting	Spit-up	Extreme Crying	Crying	Moderate fussiness	Mild fussiness	Content	Sleeping
5:00 AM										
6:00 AM										
7:00 AM										
8:00 AM										
9:00 AM										
10:00 AM										
11:00 AM										
12:00 PM										
1:00 PM										
2:00 PM										
3:00 PM										
4:00 PM										
5:00 PM										
6:00 PM										
7:00 PM										
8:00 PM										
9:00 PM										
10:00 PM										
11:00 PM										
12:00 AM										
1:00 AM										
2:00 AM										
3:00 AM										
4:00 AM										

INSTRUCTIONS: Place a mark each hour to denote what your baby's main mood was over the previous hour. Place a mark at the estimated times of spit-ups, vomiting, feedings, or diaper changes. *Make additional notes below.*

"You are all your baby will ever need"

Weekly Summary Sheet

My baby's age (in weeks):

What was the highlight (best thing that happened) this week?

Observations of my baby's crying behavior this week (e.g., how many hours on average per day did my baby cry? What time of day? Did the crying seem to correlate with certain needs or events?)

Observations of my baby's feeding and digestive patterns this week (including latching, feeding, vomiting issues, etc.):

Notes/questions from this week to remember for my pediatrician or lactation specialist:

Any lessons I need to remember from this week? (e.g., what activities did my baby seem to enjoy most?)

What I'm going to ask for more help with next week:

WEEK EIGHT

Daily Log Record

Date: _____ Day of the Week: _____

What I'm grateful for today:

How I'm going to care for/reward myself today:

How am I feeling today?

Current food trials (if any):

Number of days my baby or I have been avoiding this food:

Daily Log Chart Summary

(fill this out after today's chart on the next page is complete)

Total estimated crying time today:
Any concerns?

Total estimated sleeping time:
Any concerns?

Total number of vomiting episodes:
Any concerns?

Daily Log Chart

	Feeding	Diaper change	Vomiting	Spit-up	Extreme Crying	Crying	Moderate fussiness	Mild fussiness	Content	Sleeping
5:00 AM										
6:00 AM										
7:00 AM										
8:00 AM										
9:00 AM										
10:00 AM										
11:00 AM										
12:00 PM										
1:00 PM										
2:00 PM										
3:00 PM										
4:00 PM										
5:00 PM										
6:00 PM										
7:00 PM										
8:00 PM										
9:00 PM										
10:00 PM										
11:00 PM										
12:00 AM										
1:00 AM										
2:00 AM										
3:00 AM										
4:00 AM										

INSTRUCTIONS: Place a mark each hour to denote what your baby's main mood was over the previous hour. Place a mark at the estimated times of spit-ups, vomiting, feedings, or diaper changes. *Make additional notes below.*

Daily Log Record

Date: _____   Day of the Week: _____

What I'm grateful for today:

How I'm going to care for/reward myself today:

How am I feeling today?

Current food trials (if any):

Number of days my baby or I have been avoiding this food:

Daily Log Chart Summary

(fill this out after today's chart on the next page is complete)

Total estimated crying time today:
Any concerns?

Total estimated sleeping time:
Any concerns?

Total number of vomiting episodes:
Any concerns?

Daily Log Chart

	Feeding	Diaper change	Vomiting	Spit-up	Extreme Crying	Crying	Moderate fussiness	Mild fussiness	Content	Sleeping
5:00 AM										
6:00 AM										
7:00 AM										
8:00 AM										
9:00 AM										
10:00 AM										
11:00 AM										
12:00 PM										
1:00 PM										
2:00 PM										
3:00 PM										
4:00 PM										
5:00 PM										
6:00 PM										
7:00 PM										
8:00 PM										
9:00 PM										
10:00 PM										
11:00 PM										
12:00 AM										
1:00 AM										
2:00 AM										
3:00 AM										
4:00 AM										

INSTRUCTIONS: Place a mark each hour to denote what your baby's main mood was over the previous hour. Place a mark at the estimated times of spit-ups, vomiting, feedings, or diaper changes. *Make additional notes below.*

Daily Log Record

Date: _____   Day of the Week: _____

What I'm grateful for today:

How I'm going to care for/reward myself today:

How am I feeling today?

Current food trials (if any):

Number of days my baby or I have been avoiding this food:

Daily Log Chart Summary

(fill this out after today's chart on the next page is complete)

Total estimated crying time today:
Any concerns?

Total estimated sleeping time:
Any concerns?

Total number of vomiting episodes:
Any concerns?

Daily Log Chart

	Feeding	Diaper change	Vomiting	Spit-up	Extreme Crying	Crying	Moderate fussiness	Mild fussiness	Content	Sleeping
5:00 AM										
6:00 AM										
7:00 AM										
8:00 AM										
9:00 AM										
10:00 AM										
11:00 AM										
12:00 PM										
1:00 PM										
2:00 PM										
3:00 PM										
4:00 PM										
5:00 PM										
6:00 PM										
7:00 PM										
8:00 PM										
9:00 PM										
10:00 PM										
11:00 PM										
12:00 AM										
1:00 AM										
2:00 AM										
3:00 AM										
4:00 AM										

INSTRUCTIONS: Place a mark each hour to denote what your baby's main mood was over the previous hour. Place a mark at the estimated times of spit-ups, vomiting, feedings, or diaper changes. *Make additional notes below.*

Daily Log Record

Date: _____ Day of the Week: _____

What I'm grateful for today:

How I'm going to care for/reward myself today:

How am I feeling today?

Current food trials (if any):

Number of days my baby or I have been avoiding this food:

Daily Log Chart Summary

(fill this out after today's chart on the next page is complete)

Total estimated crying time today:
Any concerns?

Total estimated sleeping time:
Any concerns?

Total number of vomiting episodes:
Any concerns?

DAILY LOG CHART

	Feeding	Diaper change	Vomiting	Spit-up	Extreme Crying	Crying	Moderate fussiness	Mild fussiness	Content	Sleeping
5:00 AM										
6:00 AM										
7:00 AM										
8:00 AM										
9:00 AM										
10:00 AM										
11:00 AM										
12:00 PM										
1:00 PM										
2:00 PM										
3:00 PM										
4:00 PM										
5:00 PM										
6:00 PM										
7:00 PM										
8:00 PM										
9:00 PM										
10:00 PM										
11:00 PM										
12:00 AM										
1:00 AM										
2:00 AM										
3:00 AM										
4:00 AM										

INSTRUCTIONS: Place a mark each hour to denote what your baby's main mood was over the previous hour. Place a mark at the estimated times of spit-ups, vomiting, feedings, or diaper changes. *Make additional notes below.*

Daily Log Record

Date: _____ Day of the Week: _____

What I'm grateful for today:

How I'm going to care for/reward myself today:

How am I feeling today?

Current food trials (if any):

Number of days my baby or I have been avoiding this food:

Daily Log Chart Summary

(fill this out after today's chart on the next page is complete)

Total estimated crying time today:
Any concerns?

Total estimated sleeping time:
Any concerns?

Total number of vomiting episodes:
Any concerns?

Daily Log Chart

	Feeding	Diaper change	Vomiting	Spit-up	Extreme Crying	Crying	Moderate fussiness	Mild fussiness	Content	Sleeping
5:00 AM										
6:00 AM										
7:00 AM										
8:00 AM										
9:00 AM										
10:00 AM										
11:00 AM										
12:00 PM										
1:00 PM										
2:00 PM										
3:00 PM										
4:00 PM										
5:00 PM										
6:00 PM										
7:00 PM										
8:00 PM										
9:00 PM										
10:00 PM										
11:00 PM										
12:00 AM										
1:00 AM										
2:00 AM										
3:00 AM										
4:00 AM										

INSTRUCTIONS: Place a mark each hour to denote what your baby's main mood was over the previous hour. Place a mark at the estimated times of spit-ups, vomiting, feedings, or diaper changes. *Make additional notes below.*

DAILY LOG RECORD

Date: _____   Day of the Week: _____

What I'm grateful for today:

How I'm going to care for/reward myself today:

How am I feeling today?

Current food trials (if any):

Number of days my baby or I have been avoiding this food:

DAILY LOG CHART SUMMARY

(fill this out after today's chart on the next page is complete)

Total estimated crying time today:
Any concerns?

Total estimated sleeping time:
Any concerns?

Total number of vomiting episodes:
Any concerns?

Daily Log Chart

	Feeding	Diaper change	Vomiting	Spit-up	Extreme Crying	Crying	Moderate fussiness	Mild fussiness	Content	Sleeping
5:00 AM										
6:00 AM										
7:00 AM										
8:00 AM										
9:00 AM										
10:00 AM										
11:00 AM										
12:00 PM										
1:00 PM										
2:00 PM										
3:00 PM										
4:00 PM										
5:00 PM										
6:00 PM										
7:00 PM										
8:00 PM										
9:00 PM										
10:00 PM										
11:00 PM										
12:00 AM										
1:00 AM										
2:00 AM										
3:00 AM										
4:00 AM										

INSTRUCTIONS: Place a mark each hour to denote what your baby's main mood was over the previous hour. Place a mark at the estimated times of spit-ups, vomiting, feedings, or diaper changes. *Make additional notes below.*

Daily Log Record

Date: _____ Day of the Week: _____

What I'm grateful for today:

How I'm going to care for/reward myself today:

How am I feeling today?

Current food trials (if any):

Number of days my baby or I have been avoiding this food:

Daily Log Chart Summary

(fill this out after today's chart on the next page is complete)

Total estimated crying time today:
Any concerns?

Total estimated sleeping time:
Any concerns?

Total number of vomiting episodes:
Any concerns?

Daily Log Chart

	Feeding	Diaper change	Vomiting	Spit-up	Extreme Crying	Crying	Moderate fussiness	Mild fussiness	Content	Sleeping
5:00 AM										
6:00 AM										
7:00 AM										
8:00 AM										
9:00 AM										
10:00 AM										
11:00 AM										
12:00 PM										
1:00 PM										
2:00 PM										
3:00 PM										
4:00 PM										
5:00 PM										
6:00 PM										
7:00 PM										
8:00 PM										
9:00 PM										
10:00 PM										
11:00 PM										
12:00 AM										
1:00 AM										
2:00 AM										
3:00 AM										
4:00 AM										

INSTRUCTIONS: Place a mark each hour to denote what your baby's main mood was over the previous hour. Place a mark at the estimated times of spit-ups, vomiting, feedings, or diaper changes. *Make additional notes below.*

"Get outside – nature is the best remedy"

WEEKLY SUMMARY SHEET

My baby's age (in weeks):

What was the highlight (best thing that happened) this week?

Observations of my baby's crying behavior this week (e.g., how many hours on average per day did my baby cry? What time of day? Did the crying seem to correlate with certain needs or events?)

Observations of my baby's feeding and digestive patterns this week (including latching, feeding, vomiting issues, etc.):

Notes/questions from this week to remember for my pediatrician or lactation specialist:

Any lessons I need to remember from this week? (e.g., what activities did my baby seem to enjoy most?)

What I'm going to ask for more help with next week:

WEEK NINE

DAILY LOG RECORD

Date: _____   Day of the Week: _____

What I'm grateful for today:

How I'm going to care for/reward myself today:

How am I feeling today?

Current food trials (if any):

Number of days my baby or I have been avoiding this food:

DAILY LOG CHART SUMMARY

(fill this out after today's chart on the next page is complete)

Total estimated crying time today:
Any concerns?

Total estimated sleeping time:
Any concerns?

Total number of vomiting episodes:
Any concerns?

Daily Log Chart

	Feeding	Diaper change	Vomiting	Spit-up	Extreme Crying	Crying	Moderate fussiness	Mild fussiness	Content	Sleeping
5:00 AM										
6:00 AM										
7:00 AM										
8:00 AM										
9:00 AM										
10:00 AM										
11:00 AM										
12:00 PM										
1:00 PM										
2:00 PM										
3:00 PM										
4:00 PM										
5:00 PM										
6:00 PM										
7:00 PM										
8:00 PM										
9:00 PM										
10:00 PM										
11:00 PM										
12:00 AM										
1:00 AM										
2:00 AM										
3:00 AM										
4:00 AM										

INSTRUCTIONS: Place a mark each hour to denote what your baby's main mood was over the previous hour. Place a mark at the estimated times of spit-ups, vomiting, feedings, or diaper changes. *Make additional notes below.*

DAILY LOG RECORD

Date: _____ Day of the Week: _____

What I'm grateful for today:

How I'm going to care for/reward myself today:

How am I feeling today?

Current food trials (if any):

Number of days my baby or I have been avoiding this food:

DAILY LOG CHART SUMMARY

(fill this out after today's chart on the next page is complete)

Total estimated crying time today:
Any concerns?

Total estimated sleeping time:
Any concerns?

Total number of vomiting episodes:
Any concerns?

DAILY LOG CHART

	Feeding	Diaper change	Vomiting	Spit-up	Extreme Crying	Crying	Moderate fussiness	Mild fussiness	Content	Sleeping
5:00 AM										
6:00 AM										
7:00 AM										
8:00 AM										
9:00 AM										
10:00 AM										
11:00 AM										
12:00 PM										
1:00 PM										
2:00 PM										
3:00 PM										
4:00 PM										
5:00 PM										
6:00 PM										
7:00 PM										
8:00 PM										
9:00 PM										
10:00 PM										
11:00 PM										
12:00 AM										
1:00 AM										
2:00 AM										
3:00 AM										
4:00 AM										

INSTRUCTIONS: Place a mark each hour to denote what your baby's main mood was over the previous hour. Place a mark at the estimated times of spit-ups, vomiting, feedings, or diaper changes. *Make additional notes below.*

DAILY LOG RECORD

Date: _____   Day of the Week: _____

What I'm grateful for today:

How I'm going to care for/reward myself today:

How am I feeling today?

Current food trials (if any):

Number of days my baby or I have been avoiding this food:

DAILY LOG CHART SUMMARY

(fill this out after today's chart on the next page is complete)

Total estimated crying time today:
Any concerns?

Total estimated sleeping time:
Any concerns?

Total number of vomiting episodes:
Any concerns?

Daily Log Chart

	Feeding	Diaper change	Vomiting	Spit-up	Extreme Crying	Crying	Moderate fussiness	Mild fussiness	Content	Sleeping
5:00 AM										
6:00 AM										
7:00 AM										
8:00 AM										
9:00 AM										
10:00 AM										
11:00 AM										
12:00 PM										
1:00 PM										
2:00 PM										
3:00 PM										
4:00 PM										
5:00 PM										
6:00 PM										
7:00 PM										
8:00 PM										
9:00 PM										
10:00 PM										
11:00 PM										
12:00 AM										
1:00 AM										
2:00 AM										
3:00 AM										
4:00 AM										

INSTRUCTIONS: Place a mark each hour to denote what your baby's main mood was over the previous hour. Place a mark at the estimated times of spit-ups, vomiting, feedings, or diaper changes. *Make additional notes below.*

Daily Log Record

Date: _____ Day of the Week: _____

What I'm grateful for today:

How I'm going to care for/reward myself today:

How am I feeling today?

Current food trials (if any):

Number of days my baby or I have been avoiding this food:

Daily Log Chart Summary

(fill this out after today's chart on the next page is complete)

Total estimated crying time today:
Any concerns?

Total estimated sleeping time:
Any concerns?

Total number of vomiting episodes:
Any concerns?

Daily Log Chart

	Feeding	Diaper change	Vomiting	Spit-up	Extreme Crying	Crying	Moderate fussiness	Mild fussiness	Content	Sleeping
5:00 AM										
6:00 AM										
7:00 AM										
8:00 AM										
9:00 AM										
10:00 AM										
11:00 AM										
12:00 PM										
1:00 PM										
2:00 PM										
3:00 PM										
4:00 PM										
5:00 PM										
6:00 PM										
7:00 PM										
8:00 PM										
9:00 PM										
10:00 PM										
11:00 PM										
12:00 AM										
1:00 AM										
2:00 AM										
3:00 AM										
4:00 AM										

INSTRUCTIONS: Place a mark each hour to denote what your baby's main mood was over the previous hour. Place a mark at the estimated times of spit-ups, vomiting, feedings, or diaper changes. *Make additional notes below.*

DAILY LOG RECORD

Date: _____ Day of the Week: _____

What I'm grateful for today:

How I'm going to care for/reward myself today:

How am I feeling today?

Current food trials (if any):

Number of days my baby or I have been avoiding this food:

DAILY LOG CHART SUMMARY

(fill this out after today's chart on the next page is complete)

Total estimated crying time today:
Any concerns?

Total estimated sleeping time:
Any concerns?

Total number of vomiting episodes:
Any concerns?

Daily Log Chart

	Feeding	Diaper change	Vomiting	Spit-up	Extreme Crying	Crying	Moderate fussiness	Mild fussiness	Content	Sleeping
5:00 AM										
6:00 AM										
7:00 AM										
8:00 AM										
9:00 AM										
10:00 AM										
11:00 AM										
12:00 PM										
1:00 PM										
2:00 PM										
3:00 PM										
4:00 PM										
5:00 PM										
6:00 PM										
7:00 PM										
8:00 PM										
9:00 PM										
10:00 PM										
11:00 PM										
12:00 AM										
1:00 AM										
2:00 AM										
3:00 AM										
4:00 AM										

INSTRUCTIONS: Place a mark each hour to denote what your baby's main mood was over the previous hour. Place a mark at the estimated times of spit-ups, vomiting, feedings, or diaper changes. *Make additional notes below.*

Daily Log Record

Date: _____ Day of the Week: _____

What I'm grateful for today:

How I'm going to care for/reward myself today:

How am I feeling today?

Current food trials (if any):

Number of days my baby or I have been avoiding this food:

Daily Log Chart Summary

(fill this out after today's chart on the next page is complete)

Total estimated crying time today:
Any concerns?

Total estimated sleeping time:
Any concerns?

Total number of vomiting episodes:
Any concerns?

DAILY LOG CHART

	Feeding	Diaper change	Vomiting	Spit-up	Extreme Crying	Crying	Moderate fussiness	Mild fussiness	Content	Sleeping
5:00 AM										
6:00 AM										
7:00 AM										
8:00 AM										
9:00 AM										
10:00 AM										
11:00 AM										
12:00 PM										
1:00 PM										
2:00 PM										
3:00 PM										
4:00 PM										
5:00 PM										
6:00 PM										
7:00 PM										
8:00 PM										
9:00 PM										
10:00 PM										
11:00 PM										
12:00 AM										
1:00 AM										
2:00 AM										
3:00 AM										
4:00 AM										

INSTRUCTIONS: Place a mark each hour to denote what your baby's main mood was over the previous hour. Place a mark at the estimated times of spit-ups, vomiting, feedings, or diaper changes. *Make additional notes below.*

DAILY LOG RECORD

Date: _____   Day of the Week: _____

What I'm grateful for today:

How I'm going to care for/reward myself today:

How am I feeling today?

Current food trials (if any):

Number of days my baby or I have been avoiding this food:

DAILY LOG CHART SUMMARY

(fill this out after today's chart on the next page is complete)

Total estimated crying time today:
Any concerns?

Total estimated sleeping time:
Any concerns?

Total number of vomiting episodes:
Any concerns?

DAILY LOG CHART

	Feeding	Diaper change	Vomiting	Spit-up	Extreme Crying	Crying	Moderate fussiness	Mild fussiness	Content	Sleeping
5:00 AM										
6:00 AM										
7:00 AM										
8:00 AM										
9:00 AM										
10:00 AM										
11:00 AM										
12:00 PM										
1:00 PM										
2:00 PM										
3:00 PM										
4:00 PM										
5:00 PM										
6:00 PM										
7:00 PM										
8:00 PM										
9:00 PM										
10:00 PM										
11:00 PM										
12:00 AM										
1:00 AM										
2:00 AM										
3:00 AM										
4:00 AM										

INSTRUCTIONS: Place a mark each hour to denote what your baby's main mood was over the previous hour. Place a mark at the estimated times of spit-ups, vomiting, feedings, or diaper changes. *Make additional notes below.*

"You are loved"

Weekly Summary Sheet

My baby's age (in weeks):

What was the highlight (best thing that happened) this week?

Observations of my baby's crying behavior this week (e.g., how many hours on average per day did my baby cry? What time of day? Did the crying seem to correlate with certain needs or events?)

Observations of my baby's feeding and digestive patterns this week (including latching, feeding, vomiting issues, etc.):

Notes/questions from this week to remember for my pediatrician or lactation specialist:

Any lessons I need to remember from this week? (e.g., what activities did my baby seem to enjoy most?)

What I'm going to ask for more help with next week:

PEDIATRIC VISIT NOTES

PEDIATRIC VISIT NOTES

Date:_____

Pediatrician name:_____ Nurse name(s):_____

My baby's age in weeks: _____ Weight: _____ Height/Length: _____

Questions or concerns I have for the doctor:

☐ 1. For example: How I'm feeling since my baby's last visit:_____

☐ 2. _____

☐ 3. _____

☐ 4. _____

☐ 5. _____

☐ 6. _____

☐ 7. _____

Notes from the visit to remember:

Doctor Recommendations/Things to do or try before next visit:

Date of next visit:_____

Pediatric Visit Notes

Date:_____

Pediatrician name:_____ Nurse name(s): _____

My baby's age in weeks: _____ Weight: _____ Height/Length: _____

Questions or concerns I have for the doctor:

☐ 1. For example: How I'm feeling since my baby's last visit:_____

☐ 2. _____

☐ 3. _____

☐ 4. _____

☐ 5. _____

☐ 6. _____

☐ 7. _____

Notes from the visit to remember:

Doctor Recommendations/Things to do or try before next visit:

Date of next visit:_____

PEDIATRIC VISIT NOTES

Date:_____

Pediatrician name:_____ Nurse name(s):_____

My baby's age in weeks: _____ Weight: _____ Height/Length:_____

Questions or concerns I have for the doctor:

☐ 1. For example: How I'm feeling since my baby's last visit:_____

☐ 2. _____

☐ 3. _____

☐ 4. _____

☐ 5. _____

☐ 6. _____

☐ 7. _____

Notes from the visit to remember:

Doctor Recommendations/Things to do or try before next visit:

Date of next visit:_____

PEDIATRIC VISIT NOTES

Date:_____

Pediatrician name:_____ Nurse name(s):_____

My baby's age in weeks: _____ Weight: _____ Height/Length: _____

Questions or concerns I have for the doctor:

☐ 1. For example: How I'm feeling since my baby's last visit:_____

☐ 2. _____

☐ 3. _____

☐ 4. _____

☐ 5. _____

☐ 6. _____

☐ 7. _____

Notes from the visit to remember:

Doctor Recommendations/Things to do or try before next visit:

Date of next visit:_____

PEDIATRIC VISIT NOTES

Date:_____

Pediatrician name:_____ Nurse name(s):_____

My baby's age in weeks: _____ Weight: _____ Height/Length: _____

Questions or concerns I have for the doctor:

☐ 1. For example: How I'm feeling since my baby's last visit:_____

☐ 2. _____

☐ 3. _____

☐ 4. _____

☐ 5. _____

☐ 6. _____

☐ 7. _____

Notes from the visit to remember:

Doctor Recommendations/Things to do or try before next visit:

Date of next visit:_____

PEDIATRIC VISIT NOTES

Date:_____

Pediatrician name:_____ Nurse name(s):_____

My baby's age in weeks: _____ Weight: _____ Height/Length: _____

Questions or concerns I have for the doctor:

☐ 1. For example: How I'm feeling since my baby's last visit:_____

☐ 2. _____

☐ 3. _____

☐ 4. _____

☐ 5. _____

☐ 6. _____

☐ 7. _____

Notes from the visit to remember:

Doctor Recommendations/Things to do or try before next visit:

Date of next visit:_____

PEDIATRIC VISIT NOTES

Date:_____

Pediatrician name:_____ Nurse name(s):_____

My baby's age in weeks: _____ Weight: _____ Height/Length: _____

Questions or concerns I have for the doctor:

☐ 1. For example: How I'm feeling since my baby's last visit:_____

☐ 2. _____

☐ 3. _____

☐ 4. _____

☐ 5. _____

☐ 6. _____

☐ 7. _____

Notes from the visit to remember:

Doctor Recommendations/Things to do or try before next visit:

Date of next visit:_____

Pediatric Visit Notes

Date:_____

Pediatrician name:_____ Nurse name(s):_____

My baby's age in weeks: _____ Weight: _____ Height/Length: _____

Questions or concerns I have for the doctor:

☐ 1. For example: How I'm feeling since my baby's last visit:_____

☐ 2. _____

☐ 3. _____

☐ 4. _____

☐ 5. _____

☐ 6. _____

☐ 7. _____

Notes from the visit to remember:

Doctor Recommendations/Things to do or try before next visit:

Date of next visit:_____

ESSENTIAL CRYING BABY BOOK TIPS FOR WHEN YOUR BABY WON'T STOP CRYING...

1. **Breathe:** Take a moment to collect yourself, take a deep breath, know that you and your baby are going to be OK.

2. **Think:** Go through the basics. (Is it time for a feeding, diaper change, burping, or a nap?)

3. **Soothe:** If the basics are covered, try soothing (e.g., swaying, gentle bouncing, vibrating baby seat, car ride, take a walk outside with a stroller or carrier, white noise, pacifier, swaddling).

   - Give each technique at least 5 minutes to work before moving on to the next.

   - Do not take it personally if soothing doesn't work, it's not your or your baby's fault.

4. **Rest:** Call a trusted friend or family member to relieve you when your energy is low, take turns with your spouse while the other takes a walk or a shower, or take a 5 minute break in a separate room from your baby. It is OK to walk away from your baby when you need a break!

   - Be sure your baby is in a safe place such as their crib when left in a room alone.

5. **Remind:** Remind yourself you are an amazing, loving parent. The crying is not your fault.

6. **Reward:** Care for yourself with rewards such as warm baths or massages, you need it.

7. **Colic helpline:** Never feel ashamed to ask for help. It takes a village to raise a baby!

24-Hour Parent Helpline: 1-888-435-7553
Crying Baby Hotline: 1-866-243-2229
Fussy Baby Warmline: 1-888-431-BABY

Be sure to consult with your pediatrician to ensure your baby's crying is not related to any underlying medical condition. Talk to your pediatrician, doctor, family or friends about how you are feeling; don't try to bear the emotional burden of colic alone.

Keep a log of when your baby is awake, asleep, eating, and crying. Talk with your child's doctor about these behaviors to help troubleshoot causes for your baby's crying.

Journal Pages

How I'm feeling (my fears, joys, insecurities, concerns, frustrations) about caring for my baby:

Journal Pages

How I'm feeling (my fears, joys, insecurities, concerns, frustrations) about caring for my baby:

_____

_____

_____

_____

_____

_____

_____

_____

_____

_____

_____

_____

_____

_____

_____

_____

_____

_____

_____

_____

_____

_____

_____

_____

_____

_____

JOURNAL PAGES

How I'm feeling (my fears, joys, insecurities, concerns, frustrations) about caring for my baby:

_____

_____

_____

_____

_____

_____

_____

_____

_____

_____

_____

_____

_____

_____

_____

_____

_____

_____

_____

_____

_____

_____

_____

_____

_____

JOURNAL PAGES

How I'm feeling (my fears, joys, insecurities, concerns, frustrations) about caring for my baby:

_____

_____

_____

_____

_____

_____

_____

_____

_____

_____

_____

_____

_____

_____

_____

_____

_____

_____

_____

_____

_____

_____

_____

_____

_____

_____

_____

JOURNAL PAGES

How I'm feeling (my fears, joys, insecurities, concerns, frustrations) about caring for my baby:

_____

_____

_____

_____

_____

_____

_____

_____

_____

_____

_____

_____

_____

_____

_____

_____

_____

_____

_____

_____

_____

_____

_____

_____

_____

_____

_____

_____

Journal Pages

How I'm feeling (my fears, joys, insecurities, concerns, frustrations) about caring for my baby:

_____

_____

_____

_____

_____

_____

_____

_____

_____

_____

_____

_____

_____

_____

_____

_____

_____

_____

_____

_____

_____

_____

_____

_____

_____

_____

Journal Pages

How I'm feeling (my fears, joys, insecurities, concerns, frustrations) about caring for my baby:

_____

_____

_____

_____

_____

_____

_____

_____

_____

_____

_____

_____

_____

_____

_____

_____

_____

_____

_____

_____

_____

_____

_____

_____

_____

_____

JOURNAL PAGES

How I'm feeling (my fears, joys, insecurities, concerns, frustrations) about caring for my baby:

_____

_____

_____

_____

_____

_____

_____

_____

_____

_____

_____

_____

_____

_____

_____

_____

_____

_____

_____

_____

_____

_____

_____

_____

_____

Journal Pages

How I'm feeling (my fears, joys, insecurities, concerns, frustrations) about caring for my baby:

_____

_____

_____

_____

_____

_____

_____

_____

_____

_____

_____

_____

_____

_____

_____

_____

_____

_____

_____

_____

_____

_____

_____

_____

_____

_____

_____

JOURNAL PAGES

How I'm feeling (my fears, joys, insecurities, concerns, frustrations) about caring for my baby:

_____

_____

_____

_____

_____

_____

_____

_____

_____

_____

_____

_____

_____

_____

_____

_____

_____

_____

_____

_____

_____

_____

_____

_____

_____

_____

_____

_____

Extra Notes

Extra Notes

My Story and
The Essential Crying Baby Book and *Workbook*

There was a time when I looked at my 6-month-old baby, and felt completely disconnected from her. You see, when she was just two and a half weeks old, she began crying a lot. It kept getting louder to the point where her screams constantly filled the air regardless of what I did. I tried every recommendation by our pediatrician – food trials, soothing techniques, simethicone, chamomile tea, antacids – *everything*. Nothing worked. I was desperate for help and support – but I never asked for it. I feared being judged as a bad mother. I felt ashamed for not being happy given that my baby was healthy. So I suffered in silence – feeling helpless, desperate, and isolated for months.

The days, nights, and weeks ran together and it was difficult for me to keep track of her feedings, her crying episodes and how long they were really lasting, and the effectiveness of the food trials I was conducting under my pediatrician's advice. When it came time for my daughter's doctor visits, I would struggle to remember all the questions I had for him.

Even after the colic ended, the emotional trauma from the crying left me disconnected from my baby. I had to learn how to break down the wall between us. Through intense scientific research, I learned that colic and extreme fussiness can have a long-lasting impact on the mother-child relationship without the right kind of support. Thus I decided to share my research findings regarding causes, treatments, and emotional impacts of infant colic in my new book, *The Essential Crying Baby Book: Support and Resources to Help You Cope With Colic and Calm Your Fussy Baby*, aimed to help other mothers and fathers struggling with a colicky or extremely fussy baby. *The Essential Crying Baby Workbook* helps parents who are trying to get a better handle on their fussy baby's behavioral patterns for themselves and for discussions with their pediatrician, and serves as a reminder for self-care and self-compassion during these challenging times.

If you or someone you know is struggling with a baby that cries more than usual, please check out our website at www.essentialcryingbabybook.com and join our **Community**.

With Love,

Kristi Smith

About the Author

DR. KRISTINE SMITH is a certified Health and Wellness Coach, research scientist, speaker and author. Kristine grew up in the small town of Jonesboro in Downeast coastal Maine. She studied Biology at Wheaton College, Massachusetts before obtaining her veterinary medical degree from Tufts University. Smith completed a residency at the Bronx Zoo in New York, providing medical care for all creatures great and small before becoming an international wildlife veterinarian. Her career has since broadened to focus on global public health for nearly a decade, traveling and working throughout Africa, Asia, and Latin America. Kristine partnered with and led workshops for United Nations agencies such as the World Health Organization, Food and Agriculture Organization, and the World Bank, as well as US agencies such as the Centers for Disease Control and Prevention. Smith has given speeches for the International Meeting for Emerging Diseases, Princeton University, and the World Conservation Congress, among others. Smith has contributed to books on the human-animal bond and disease, and published in many peer-reviewed scientific journals including the *Journal of Pediatric Health Care*. Dr. Smith is currently a certified health and wellness coach and focuses on individual health and behavior choices that support overall well-being. Her interests lie in the topics of maternal mental health, judgement-free parenting, healthy aging and the human-animal-environmental bond and health connections. Kristine and her husband Jason had their first daughter, Katiya, in 2009, who suffered from severe colic for four months. They welcomed a second daughter, Keira, in 2012. Smith and her family currently live in Connecticut with their three adopted "fur babies" (two cats and an Australian Shepherd).

www.ingramcontent.com/pod-product-compliance
Lightning Source LLC
Chambersburg PA
CBHW062041090426
42740CB00016B/2983